Thanks for Nothing

The Gross Injustice of the Second Judicial District Court of Washoe County – Family Court Division

A mother's journey through the family courts and the abhorrent conclusion to a long drawn out divorce case.

I0490292

"Human progress is neither automatic nor inevitable... Every step toward the goal of justice requires sacrifice, suffering, and struggle; the tireless exertions and passionate concern of dedicated individuals."

— Martin Luther King, Jr.

Words from the heart

My mother told me that when I felt like I was at my lowest point possible during all of this to remember one thing, this is for the children. She said many times during the past 17 years that if only the ex-husband could love his son as much as he hated me, things would be drastically different.

As a mother, my mom could see the pain in my heart as the years passed by and the battles became more and more hurtful to my soul, but she was strong for me, for my son, and for the purpose that was behind every decision I made as a mother myself. Without her, I am unsure that I would have survived all of this intact. It was not easy for her as she sat through every court hearing, listening to me read every court paper to her, but she knew her daughter and her grandson needed some security. It is with this, that I thank her, from every piece of my soul, for her courage, her strength, and her support…

My attorney, has undoubtedly dealt with her own personal battles during the 17 years of this case. I cannot thank her enough for being there to provide her own knowledge, stability, and generosity. Without her, I would be in a much worse position than I am now. There were hard decisions to make and while she may not have personally agreed with them, she supported me and provided the brutal honesty that is needed. Thank you, words could never describe how grateful I am.

Dedication

I dedicate this book to the mothers and fathers who have been or are going through a divorce. With children involved, divorces are bound to get ugly, there is a lot of emotional influence when going through a divorce. I hope that my story can provide you with some solace in knowing that you are not alone, to give you the strength to go forward in a more knowledgeable way, and to give you a peek into one of the most horrendous battles I have honestly encountered.

Special Notes

All docket entries are listed from current to previous.

CHAPTER 1

2001: The Beginning

January 29, 2001 is what the divorce decree stated. After a 6-month battle and many revisions on the decree, it was finally over. The divorce decree was signed by Judge McGee, one of the first judges that I would encounter.

I finally felt the relief of many divorcees. I was free from a marriage that was an utter disaster. I could find myself again. When I received the final Divorce Decree, signed by the judge, the look of my name in its maiden form was never more beautiful. I was Meghan Bailey once again, and my long atrocious battle would soon be over.

I was horribly mistaken. The following 17 years would bring about a lot of personal feelings and would prove that there was a more deep and dark underworld of the Family Court Division. Filled with disappointment, malicious and false accusations, and pure injustice. This marks the beginning of my journey through the Washoe County Second Judicial District Court – Family Court Division along with the Washoe County District Attorney's Office – Child Support Division and the State of Nevada.

Visitation

I wanted to be as fair as possible regarding visitation, even though John had insisted on attempting to make my life miserable. The visitation schedule was ordered that John would have the child for a limited amount of time during every other weekend. There were initially no overnight stays because he was not in a safe and secure place. However, once he obtained a safe and secure home, visitations would include overnight stays. John would receive Adam on his birthday, Father's Day, and holidays would be rotated. Adam was only a year and a half old during this time. I made the mistake of several parents in thinking that this divorce would not affect him as much as older children. It was a mistake that I am constantly reminded of.

Later I would realize that what John lacked in interest for the child, was put towards the animosity and pure hatred that he felt for me.

Child Support

Child Support was ordered through the Washoe County District Attorney's Office, the payments were set at the normal 18% of John's income. At that time, the payment per month was set at $162.00. It was ordered that he provide proof of income every six months and that he was to provide medical insurance on the child.

Personal Debt

John was ordered to pay back monies owed. While married, John had several unpaid fines in California and Nevada, resulting in the suspension of his license. For him to work, it was necessary to pay off these debts so that he could get his license back. I had money from a previous settlement that was used. In the divorce decree, it was ordered that John pay $500.00, payable in $100.00 per month installments.

In addition to this debt, it was ordered that other debts shared would be divided equally between both of us. That never happened, in the end it was up to me to carry the burden and pay for these debts myself and with the help of my parents. John was also required to pay $26.00 on medical bills for Adam. He never made that payment.

During 2001, I attended the Western Nevada Peace Officer's Academy. I wanted my son to be proud of his mother. I knew that whatever I did, directly affected him in every way. Being a single mother was going to be hard, but I was determined to make our lives better.

Around August, 2001… There was an incident at my parent's house, it was decided that I should move out. I did not have anywhere else to go but to stay with a few friends in Las Vegas. I didn't think it would be responsible to drag my son down there, I didn't know much of where I would be staying and I didn't know if it would be suitable for my son. I called John and explained what was going on and asked him if it would be alright if Adam stayed with my parents for the time being. He agreed, since neither of us had our affairs in order, it was the more responsible decision. I crouched down and kissed my son goodbye, the embrace was not long enough. I was young and needed a good dose of reality, I would get that in Las Vegas, more than my fair share. And my son? He would be safe. He was far too young to know any better. I would call him every single day for the 6 months that I spent in Las Vegas. John would later lead others to believe that I was there for far longer and for far more sinister reasons. The fallacy of abandonment was far from accurate.

I came back for Christmas and at the first sight of my son, I broke down. I could not believe how much he had grown. And all though we talked every day on the phone when I walked into my mother's kitchen that cold day in December, my son, looked at me like I was a stranger. I knew that I needed to come home, he needed his mother.

You see, I haven't been the perfect mom, I will never claim to be. I have always acted with my children's best interests in mind. And for that, I live with no regrets.

Child Support

Just before I left for Las Vegas, Nevada in 2001, I had made a call to the child support office and spoke with Yolanda, a replacement for the previous case worker Gwen. The purpose of this phone call was to ask if I could have the child support checks put in my mother's name, since she would be the one caring for my son. This was not acceptable and I decided to keep the address at my parents and have the checks sent there. During this time John's wages were being garnished and I was receiving regular child support payments.

221. 2530 - Notice of Entry of Decree	31- Jan- 2001	*Extra Text:*	
223. 1540 - Decree of Divorce	30- Jan- 2001	*Extra Text: DECREE OF DIVORCE MARITAL SETTLEMENT AGREEMENT DATED 1/17/2001 AS EXHIBIT "A" IS APPROVED AND RATIFIED BY THE COURT. MEGHAN RESTORED TO HER MAIDEN NAME, MEGHAN ALISA BAILEY.*	

CHAPTER 2

2002

All was quiet in 2002, yet there was sadness in the way things were headed. I had moved back to Reno and was in a cozy one-bedroom apartment. Adam would spend much of his time with me. We would go to the parks, chase ducks at the lake, go shopping at the mall, it was all about fun and keeping his mind busy! As things got better, I ended up moving back into my parent's home with Adam. During the 6 months that I spent in Las Vegas, John had only visited Adam once. Things did not improve on that end once I had moved back.

My son was just old enough to start asking the difficult questions. I had to decide, do I try to explain to him at just 3 years old why his father would not call, would not answer, and was not around to visit? I started covering for John during this time. It was not an easy thing to do since I must admit there was some animosity on my end.

When it came time for John to have his visitation, I was met with *"Oh, I am busy this weekend."* Other times the phone calls would be ignored. I would leave countless messages asking John if he would like to see Adam. The replies were few and far between.

I found myself angry, frustrated, and hurt that no matter how many times I called John to see if he would be taking his son that weekend, he would ignore the calls or simply provide an excuse as to why it "wasn't the right time".

And although John was basically non-existent during this time, Adam and I managed to go on about our lives. We simply just had fun. Deep down inside, I was disgusted with John, hurt, and could not fathom why a father would choose to ignore the fact that he had a son.

I fought for my son and for John to have some relationship, however John was uninterested. I received no help other than one pack of diapers and a $25.00 money order. Child support was non-existent and nothing was being done about it.

Adam and I were still living with my parents during this time. While I made some cash doing a few jobs here and there, it was never enough to "make it" on our own. Adam's birthday came and went, there was no contact with John. There was only one birthday that John made an appearance at, it was Adam's first birthday. Of course, I was filled with frustration.

At this time, I had no idea the extent of John's maliciousness. Only after I had moved on and met my second husband in May of 2003 did the situation get progressively worse. The true colors started to show, and the color was red.

Child Support

In December of 2002 I had spoken with Yolanda again regarding my child support case. This time I was seeking modification. In the divorce decree, John was ordered to provide proof of employment every six months. This happened on only two occasions. I had just received a paycheck stub from John and noticed that I was getting 18% of an $8.00 an hour job, this new paycheck stub would provide $288.00 a month in child support at the rate of 18%.

After an argument with John over his refusal of providing proof of employment, he hung up. A short while later I had received a phone call from Yolanda stating that she had spoken with John. He denied the most recent paycheck stub and I asked the caseworker if she would like me to fax the stub over to her. Imagine my surprise when she stated that "there was no need for it".

A few days went by and my mother had received a phone call from the Washoe County District Attorney's office, wanting to know the specifics of the dates that I was in Las Vegas. They wanted to know if the child support that was paid during that time was going towards my son.

CHAPTER 3

2003: A new beginning

In May of 2003 I met who would later become my second husband. We enjoyed our time together but knew that he would eventually have to return to Phoenix, AZ where he lived. That summer I realized a lot about myself and where I wanted my son and me to be. He finally asked me while sitting at the bar in the local Applebee's if my son and I would move to Phoenix with him. I replied that I had some issues I needed to work out and get approval from the courts for relocation.

Things were set into motion at that time, and I was again, happy. My son and Ken bonded immediately once they met, Ken showered Adam in gifts and recognized his worn-out shoes on their first meet. Ken took us to the mall and bought Adam a brand-new set of sneakers. At that moment, I realized that this man would be more of a father to my son, than his own biological one could ever be. My son and I were accepted by this man.

Shortly after, I filed a Motion for Relocation with the Second Judicial District Court in Washoe County. I supplied information and logical reasoning why this move would benefit Adam and me. Unfortunately, John who had been non-existent would also have his say-so. I never understood, and honestly still do not understand why a person who made clear they wanted no involvement in the child previously, could have a say in where that child moved. If they did not care in the beginning, why would they care now? Among the many ridiculous claims from John as to why I should not be allowed to relocate, one of them was the fact that I would be a stay-at-home mother. John believed this would not be conducive to Adam's health.

In the end, I won my right to relocate to Phoenix, Arizona. We were on the road, the three of us in August of 2003. We packed up our little U-Haul trailer and made the 12-hour drive to our new home. With promise of a new beginning, we were thrilled. Adam was beyond happy and the bonding between him and Ken remained strong and grew every day thereafter.

After going through the issue with Relocation and John condemning it, I filed an Order to Show Cause against John. I was appearing in Proper Person (Pro Per) My mother has always told me that what is right is right, what is wrong is wrong. John had refused to pay for unpaid medical expenses and the personal debt. Of course, I could have just let it go, but in the end, we must all be held accountable.

The Order went to a hearing, Judge McGee was presiding and ordered in my favor in the amount of $592.31. Medical bills would be received through wage withholding and the personal debt was my responsibility to follow through on.

Finally, I felt as if this court would hold John accountable, until I went to serve the order. I was told the order could not be followed since it was not typed up correctly. In turn, John would never be ordered to pay back the monies owed and garnishment would never take place. I was told to refile and return to court to ask Judge McGee to write an order on this matter that could be followed. I decided not to pursue this matter any further, knowing I would likely never see the money.

Adam at 4 years old was open to almost anything, as long as it involved Sponge Bob, a McDonald's Happy Meal, and love. At that age, it was up to me to make sure that he spoke with his dad on a weekly basis. I remember many, many times where the phone would ring and ring, no answer. Adam would look down and walk away. One evening after about two months of trying to contact his father, Adam asked me, *"Why doesn't Dad answer his phone?"* I would cover for John and tell Adam that maybe he was busy, but he would get his message and call him back for sure. Of course, he never did. During the phone calls that did take place between the two, they were short.

At this time, visitation was during Spring Break, the whole month of June, and Thanksgiving. Ken and I would drive Adam to Las Vegas and meet John for the transfer. Adam was always excited to get away and see his father on the way there. When we would pick Adam up, he was melancholy, sad, sometimes even angry. But the worst was when he would repeat what his father had told him.

Ken and I would sit in front, lips tight, and try to brush it off. This occurred every time Adam would return from his father's. The animosity from Adam's father was intense and would only escalate as the years passed on.

For two years Ken and I met John in Las Vegas for the transfer. During one meeting, Ken finally approached John and explained to him what Adam was feeling and saying, and that if John continued to do this, he wouldn't be hurting us, but he would be hurting Adam. John continued to deny such talks with his son and simply showed no care at all.

I had met Jane with an open-mind, knowing that she would be a big part of Adam's life from here on out. However, I did not expect that she would be one of the biggest antagonizer in this saga. The few times that I had spoken with Jane, she professed that she didn't want to be "in the middle" of John and I's court battles, but to just be there for my son Adam. Fair enough.

Child Support

On March 6, 2003, I had enough of the bias from the Washoe County District Attorney's Office. As they were the handlers of my child support case, it became increasingly difficult to work with them for any type of resolution. I attempted to write a letter to Lucille Knight, the supervisor at that time.

On March 5, 2003, I received a phone call from Yolanda, she stated that she had received the information regarding the dates while I was in Las Vegas and how the child support monies were spent, but that she saw no need in modifying the current support. Instead she promptly notified me that I was going to be audited by their office.

The phone calls received from Yolanda proved to be very bias towards John and filled with intimidation and harassment. I asked for a new case worker and recommended that "Yolanda" take a few courses on work ethics.

On April 18, 2003, I filed a Motion to Modify Support Order asking that John's child support be increased to $288.00 per month.

On July 1, 2003, I received a letter stating that a hearing had been set to Determine Arrears for August 14, 2003. It would be the last hearing I would attend for the Washoe County District Attorney's office regarding my child support case.

183. 3355 - Ord to Show Cause	22-Dec-2003	*Extra Text: SET FOR 1-29-04 AT 3:00 PM*
184. 3860 - Request for Submission	03-Dec-2003	*Extra Text: DOCUMENT TITLE: APPLICATION FOR ORDER TO SHOW CAUSE REGARDING CONTEMPT PARTY SUBMITTING: JOHN DOE DATE SUBMITTED: 12/4/03 SUBMITTED BY: LMATHEUS DATE RECEIVED JUDGE'S OFFICE:*
185. 1245 - Application Ord Show Cause	03-Dec-2003	*Extra Text:*
186. 2700 - Ord After Hearing...	20-Nov-2003	*Extra Text: ORDER AFTER HEARING: JUDGMENT IN FAVOR OF PLAINTIFF IN THE SUM OF $592.31. PLAINTIFF'S REQUEST FOR DAYCARE WILL NOT BE GRANTED AND MEDICAL BILLS WILL BE RECEIVED THROUGH WAGE WITHHOLDING SHALL BE PLTF'S RESPONSIBILITY TO FOLLOW THROUGH ON.*
187. F220 - Decision with Hearing	18-Nov-2003	*Extra Text:*
189. 3370 - Order ...	28-Oct-2003	*Extra Text: ORDER GRANTING TELEPHONIC APPEARANCE ON 11/18/2003 AT 1:25 PM*
191. 3860 - Request for Submission	24-Oct-2003	*Extra Text: DOCUMENT TITLE: EX PARTE MOTION FOR PERMISSION TO HAVE A TELEPHONE CONFERENCE HEARING FOR THE ORDER TO SHOW CAUSE HEARING SCHEDULED FOR OCTOBER 28, 2003 @ 3:00 p.m. PARTY SUBMITTING: MEGHAN ALISA BAILEY, PRO PER DATE*

		SUBMITTED: 10-24-03 SUBMITTED BY: A. SULLIVAN DATE RECEIVED JUDGE'S OFFICE:
193. 1067 - Affidavit of Service	23-Sep-2003	*Extra Text: Application for Order to Show Cause Regarding Contempt, Order to Show Cause Regarding Contempt, Request for Submission of Application for Order to Show Cause - Served on John Doe on 9/17/03*
194. 3355 - Ord to Show Cause	12-Sep-2003	*Extra Text: ORDER TO SHOW CAUASE REGARDING CONTEMPT OCTOBER 28, 2003 AT 3PM IN D-2*
199. 3860 - Request for Submission	10-Sep-2003	*Extra Text: DOCUMENT TITLE: ORDER TO SHOW CAUSE PARTY SUBMITTING: MEGHAN BAILEY DATE SUBMITTED: 9/10/03 SUBMITTED BY: CPARSLEY DATE RECEIVED JUDGE'S OFFICE:*
200. 1245 - Application Ord Show Cause	10-Sep-2003	*Extra Text:*
201. 2700 - Ord After Hearing...	09-Sep-2003	*Extra Text: PLAINTIFFS MOTION TO RELOCATE IS GRANTED. ORDER IS EFFECTIVE NINC PRO TUNC TO HEARING DATE OF 8/21/03 .*
202. F220 - Decision With Hearing	21-Aug-2003	*Extra Text:*
203. MIN - ***Minutes	21-Aug-2003	*Extra Text: ORDER TO SHOW CAUSE*
204. 3370 - Order ...	06-Aug-2003	*Extra Text: ORDER VACATING & RESETTING HEARING HEARING RESET TO 8/21/03 AT 11PM D-2*
206. 3370 - Order ...	28-Jul-2003	*Extra Text: ORDER SETTING HEARING ON MOTION TO RELOCATE*
207. 3355 - Ord to	23-	*Extra Text: ORDER TO SHOW*

Show Cause	Jul-2003	*CAUSE REGARDING CONTEMPT*
209. 3860 - Request for Submission	16-Jul-2003	*Extra Text: DOCUMENT TITLE: MOTION FOR PERMISSION TO RELOCATE PARTY SUBMITTING: MEGHAN ALISA BAILEY DATE SUBMITTED: 07/17/03 SUBMITTED BY: MPURDY DATE RECEIVED JUDGE'S OFFICE:*
210. 3795 - Reply...	16-Jul-2003	*Extra Text: REPLY TO RESPONSE TO MOTION*
212. 1245 - Application Ord Show Cause	11-Jul-2003	*Extra Text:*
213. 3880 - Response...	11-Jul-2003	*Extra Text: TO MOTION*
215. 3860 - Request for Submission	11-Jul-2003	*Extra Text: DOCUMENT TITLE: APPLICATION FOR ORDER TO SHOW CAUSE REGARDING CONTEMPT PARTY SUBMITTING: JOHN DOE DATE SUBMITTED: 7-11-03 SUBMITTED BY: A. SULLIVAN DATE RECEIVED JUDGE'S OFFICE:*
216. $1985 - **$Motion/Opposition Notice	11-Jul-2003	*Extra Text: JOHN DOE*
219. $1985 - **$Motion/Opposition Notice	02-Jul-2003	*Extra Text: MEGHAN ALISA BAILEY*
220. 2490 - Motion ...	02-Jul-2003	*Extra Text: MEGHAN ALISA BAILEY*

CHAPTER 4

2004

I had met John and Jane at the mall for the transfer of Adam for visitation. I was never comfortable with meeting John alone so my mother came along with me for support. John and Jane were already waiting in the parking lot when we pulled up. As we walked over and Adam was saying his goodbyes to Grandma and myself, Jane stormed over and handed me an envelope. With a sneer, she said *"you've been served"*. I was taken back by this, not that I was surprised that I was being served with more court documents, but that they thought this was the perfect time to do this. In front of our son, during a transfer, and that sneer… I would never forget that. For someone who professed that she would not be "in the middle", this sure seemed like she put herself there. This was a motion John had filed claiming that I had refused to allow him to see Adam, and because I had vented my frustrations on my own personal website.

I was improperly served with another Motion by Jane the day of the hearing inside the courthouse, it was heard by Judge McGee despite my testimony that I had just been served with this document just minutes before the start of the hearing. That's when I realized that she was involved even though she stated several times that she was not and did not want anything to do with any of the legalities. I realized at this time, this woman was and would be playing a major role in the deception and destruction of our family. During this hearing, Judge McGee stated that I was not held in contempt, however it was my fault that things were not going as planned because I was the one who moved. It was my responsibility to facilitate the visitations. This is where I realized that the chances of this court ever holding John responsible, was rapidly diminishing.

Judge McGee ordered that the courts would monitor my website and that if I wrote anything that described John in any way, he would give custody over to John.

John filed contempt of court on me stating that I had been showing Adam nude photos of myself, the evidence was false and knowingly John submitted that evidence. My attorney was brought back onto the case because of Judge McGee's threat of handing custody to John as well as nude photographs. The case was dropped after it was exposed as being false.

Co-parenting with John was difficult on many levels, mainly because he showed absolutely no interest in the betterment of Adam. I was very generous in the divorce terms, allowing John one extra weekend per month with Adam, it would be on John's expense and would have to take place in Arizona. He accepted only one weekend in 8 years. During the time that Adam live in Arizona with me, John would refuse to allow Adam to participate in any sport activities. Adam had shown a lot of interest in baseball, karate, swimming, and other activities, but with the threats of more litigation from John and his refusal in helping to pay for anything, I was limited in what I could do for Adam. During Adam's short time participating and competing in karate and Brazilian Jiu Jitsu, he did amazing. Adam won many medals in competitions and skipped belt classes during testing. Despite the encouragement from teachers and coaches, John would not allow any of it.

Adam would get Christmas and birthday gifts at his dad's but was never allowed to bring them back home with him to Arizona. John continuously showed the need to control every aspect of Adam's life, even when he was home in Arizona.

I remember countless times when John would complain that I would not let him see Adam, but he himself chose not to take advantage of the extra time given. For one summer visitation, I allowed Adam to stay with his father for the entire month of June as court ordered, but also the month of July as well. This was the first time Adam had spent a birthday with his father. I did this out of kindness and compassion for Adam. It backfired like all other times where I had been very generous with John.

A few times, John even stated that he would not be sending Adam back, finally with the threat of calling the Sheriff's Department, John conceded and sent Adam back home.

It seemed as if it was always a fight, and in truth, it was. It was a fight for justice, and a fight for the best interests of the child.

Unfortunately, the one venue that could provide this, failed in many ways and continues to fail. My life was consumed by this. I was always documenting something, phone calls, visitations, even conversations. I fell into this habit of keeping every little note, piece of paper, mail. It was ridiculous. My life was and would be for the next several years be documented on paper. Everything needed to be in writing. John would use any means necessary to set me up and lead me into another deception of his.

158. 2540 - Notice of Entry of Ord	28-Jul-2004	*Extra Text:*
160. 3370 - Order ...	27-Jul-2004	*Extra Text: ORDER RE: CHILD CUSTODY & VISITATION*
162. 3860 - Request for Submission	20-Jul-2004	*Extra Text: DOCUMENT TITLE: MOTION REQUESTING INTERLOCUTORY ORDER OF 9/9/03 BE MADE PERMANENT ORDER IN THE CASE DATE SUBMITTED: 7/21/04 SUBMITTED BY: LMATHEUS DATE RECEIVED JUDGE'S OFFICE:*
163. 3835 - Report...	20-May-2004	*Extra Text: STATUS REPORT RE: RELOCATION OF MINOR CHILD MOTION REQUESTING INTERLOCUTORY ORDER OF 9/9/03 BE MADE PERMANENT ORDER IN THE CASE*
164. 2540 - Notice of Entry of Ord	22-Apr-2004	*Extra Text:*
165. 2700 - Ord After Hearing...	20-Apr-2004	*Extra Text: PLAINTIFF IS NOT HELD IN CONTEMPT OF THE COURT'S PREVIOUS ORDER.*
166. MIN - ***Minutes	01-Mar-2004	*Extra Text: ORDER TO SHOW CAUSE*
169. 3370 - Order ...	20-Feb-2004	*Extra Text: Order to Show Cause (UNABLE TO IMAGE - DOCUMENT NOT IN FILE)*
170. 3355 - Ord to Show Cause	20-Feb-2004	*Extra Text: MARCH 1, 2004 AT 10AM IN D-2*
171. 3370 - Order ...	20-Feb-2004	*Extra Text: Order to Show Cause (UNABLE TO IMAGE - DOCUMENT NOT IN FILE)*
172. 3860 - Request for Submission	13-Feb-2004	*Extra Text: DOCUMENT TITLE: APPLICATION FOR ORDER TO SHOW CAUSE PARTY SUBMITTING: MEGHAN ALISA BAILEY DATE SUBMITTED: 2-13-04*

		SUBMITTED BY: A. MARTINEZ DATE RECEIVED JUDGE'S OFFICE:
173. 1245 - Application Ord Show Cause	13-Feb-2004	*Extra Text: Document sealed, contains pornographic images - MPurdy - 09/15/09*
174. 2700 - Ord After Hearing...	04-Feb-2004	*Extra Text:*
176. 2840 - Ord Denying ...	27-Jan-2004	*Extra Text: ORDER DENYING EX PARTE MOTION FOR TELEPHONE HEARING*
177. 3860 - Request for Submission	27-Jan-2004	*Extra Text: DOCUMENT TITLE: EX PARTE EMERGENCY MOTION FOR TELEPHONIC HEARING PARTY SUBMITTING: MEGHAN ALISA BAILEY DATE SUBMITTED: 1-27-04 SUBMITTED BY: A.MARTINEZ DATE RECEIVED JUDGE'S OFFICE:*
178. 3355 - Ord to Show Cause	22-Jan-2004	*Extra Text: ORDER TO SHOW CASUE REGARDING CONTEMPT HEARING SET FOR JANUARY 29, 2004 AT 3PM IN D-2*
179. 1245 - Application Ord Show Cause	20-Jan-2004	*Extra Text: JOHN DOE (UNABLE TO IMAGE - DOCUMENT NOT IN FILE)*
180. 3860 - Request for Submission	20-Jan-2004	*Extra Text: (UNABLE TO IMAGE - DOCUMENT NOT IN FILE)*
181. 3860 - Request for Submission	20-Jan-2004	*Extra Text: DOCUMENT TITLE: APPLICATION FOR ORDER TO SHOW CAUSE REGARDING PARTY SUBMITTING: JOHN DOE DATE SUBMITTED: 1-20-04 SUBMITTED BY: A. MARTINEZ DATE RECEIVED JUDGE'S OFFICE:*
182. 1245 - Application Ord Show Cause	20-Jan-2004	

CHAPTER 5

All was quiet during 2005, 2006, and 2007 as far as courts went. I still dealt with the negative remarks from John, the verbal abuse over the phone, and the unwillingness to work together to solve issues. Adam was old enough that I was comfortable in purchasing "unaccompanied minor" flights, direct from Phoenix to Reno. It was both cheaper and more convenient for both John and myself. John would pay for the flight to Reno and I would pay for the flight to Arizona. Other times Adam's grandparents would make arrangements to pick Adam up in Arizona and spend a week with him at their home in Reno. They would then deliver Adam to John for his visitation.

In June 2006, I gave birth to my daughter. Through the following years, Adam was a big help with my daughter. Always eager to keep her entertained for a few minutes while I took a quick shower or cleaned a bit around the house. He loved his little sister, those two developed a very close bond. In January 2007, I was pinned between two vehicles and suffered some significant blunt force trauma. I needed a lot of help around the house. I was in rehabilitative therapy for 6 weeks, because of the accident I suffered two herniated discs, degenerative disc disease, arthritis, carpal tunnel, and hyper extended both knees. While my second husband was working, Adam had to step up to the plate. I didn't know then that this issue would later be brought up in a CPS report a couple years later.

We continued with our lives and always tried to make the most of whatever was thrown our way. I started to notice after every visit with John, Adam would become more and more distant. Adam would act out more and his relationship with my second husband was beginning to diminish. Adam started to lie and act out a lot more, he became more reclusive and defiant. I was becoming more worried that this relationship with his father was becoming more and more toxic.

CHAPTER 6

2008

This would be the year that consumed the next several years. The year which John had based his allegations of child abuse on and other lies. I haven't talked about this year, not in court and not in any other aspect. Simply, it wasn't worth discussing and I felt it best to just let John and Jane continue to show their idiocy and paranoia.

I will however, address this infamous year now… During the summer, I had met Ken's cousins once in Arkansas. They had fallen on hard times and were looking for a place to get help and start fresh. Ken had asked me if it would be ok for them to stay with us in Arizona with their two kids. Ken would try to get his cousin Randy a job at his place of employment and the cousin's wife Phoebe would work to find a job as well.

I agreed, I had received help from family and friends before when I had fallen on hard times. This was my way of paying it forward. It didn't take long to realize this was a very toxic and dangerous situation.

One day, Randy arrived at the house and was intoxicated, Phoebe was angry with him that he had been out drinking instead of working. The two got into a very physical and loud verbal fight. I ushered the kids upstairs and told them to lock the door in their bedroom. I attempted to get between the two and became a target of their rage. Ken had to take Randy down in the hallway and I had to pin Phoebe near the entry way. The Sheriff's Department was called and both Phoebe and Randy fled the area. After the Deputies had taken our statements and left, Ken decided he needed to find his cousin. After an hour, I had gotten the kids calmed down and fed, I got a call from Ken. He told me that Randy and Phoebe were going to come back, they had calmed down, and were very sorry.

I told Ken that they were not allowed to come back, there was no way I was going to allow those two in my home with my young children. They needed to find somewhere else to go. Ken was adamant about them coming back and I was very firm in my stance.

Ken had decided to choose his cousin Randy and Phoebe over his step son and daughter. I packed all the necessities we needed, grabbed Adam and my daughter and we drove to Reno, Nevada to stay with my parents. I refused to allow that kind of violent behavior around my children.

Once I got to Reno, I called John the next day. I explained that we were up in Reno with my parents, I wasn't sure how long we would be there. I let John know that Adam was there and if he wanted to see him, to just give me a call and we would set up a visitation.

In August, I made a decision to better myself. I signed up for classes at the University of Phoenix. I began my studies for my Associate's in Criminal Justice. I was excited and proud, I would be showing my son and my daughter that education is important regardless of what age. I knew that this would be a difficult road, attending college full-time while taking care of my family and keeping up with the housework, but, I also knew that it was going to be worth every moment that I needed to sacrifice with them.

So, there you have it, the HORRIBLE atrocities and abuse that happened in my home during 2008. (dripping with sarcasm) After a month or two, Ken and I reconciled, Randy and Phoebe were back in Arkansas, it was time to go back to Arizona. We had a lot of work ahead of us as a family. John would try to seize this episode as an opportunity to take Adam away from his family in Arizona.

CHAPTER 7

2009

I had wanted to keep the "peace" on many levels. I was unable to discipline Adam without some recourse from John. Usually in the form of angry voicemails or more court documents alleging some form of "atrocity". For example, taking away Adam's cell phone would be turned into me refusing John being able to talk with his son. Even though he was more than welcomed to call the house phone or my cell phone as long as he remained respectful. Any attempts to be logical or fair were met with such intense allegations and more attacks through the courts. My hands were tied. No matter how fair I would try to be, it was always thrown in my face.

In January of 2009, I was welcomed into that year by a stack of papers, John wanted custody of our nine-year-old son. I conferred with my attorney and we had drafted up a probationary custody agreement that would give John our son for one year. John turned it down, instead of getting his son for one year that June, he decided that he wanted him immediately in March. This would have ripped our son out of school in the middle of the school year. This was unacceptable in my eyes. I refused to rip Adam from his friends and family in the middle of a school year. John would have had to wait 2 months, when his visitation started. John was unwilling to work on this. Instead of waiting two more months and then starting his visitation, he allowed his ego to take over and pompously demanded his son immediately. That offer was removed immediately after John's demands.

John had been notorious for blaming his lack of contact with Adam on me. He had alleged several times that I wouldn't allow him to talk with Adam or that I was trying to keep Adam from him. I had to make sure Adam had his phone on him AT ALL TIMES. If John had called and Adam did not pick up for whatever reason, i.e. on the toilet, outside with friends, swimming, I would receive another motion alleging that I was restricting communication. Adam was a prisoner with his phone. This type of obsessive/controlling nature from John mirrored his actions in our marriage.

After those papers came, a slew of other documents was filed. John alleged that there was horrible abuse going on in my home and it was urgent that Adam be placed with him immediately. While the judge denied these custody motions, over and over again, nothing was being done with the fact that this man was already in contempt of the previous divorce decree. In fact, John was never punished for perjury even though the proof was in the many documents that were filed on my behalf. It was clear that this court would never hold John accountable. I was always defending myself from these wild allegations. As John would filed a motion, my attorney would file an opposition. John would argue anything and everything that he could. He always demanded that the TRUTH be told, even though none of his motions were ever credible and held not an ounce of proof of what he was alleging.

There were a few times where it was ridiculous at best to show up to court to defend myself against John's obsessive need to file motion after motion. John had become well known for twisting and turning things to suit his agenda. While Ken and I had to deal with years of hearing all the bad things about Mom from Adam that John and Jane would say, John would request that bad things not be said about either party. And although throughout the years John would refuse to send Adam home until the threat of the Sheriff's Office becoming involved would come up, he felt it important to ask that the child not be withheld from the other party.

John and Jane would both use whatever they could to mold Adam into what they wanted. At one point, they even bribed Adam with the ability to visit his Grandparent's more often if he lived with them. Adam's Grandparents were a large part of Adam's life, they were his "safety zone". Adam knew he would always be safe at his Grandparent's and that he could get away from the "drama". To use Adam's Grandparent's like that, was despicable and grotesque.

Adam would come home from visitations with John and Jane with a look of contempt. He would complain that his dad and Jane would share the contents of the litigation with him. Adam would come to me with questions and put me on the spot. I would grow furious that my son was being subjected to this. I had urged John and Jane both to stop with this, it was only causing more friction in the home and disrupting Adam's life. They did not care.

> 7.   The Court finds that Defendant discussed the litigation with the minor child. It is the goal of the Court to prevent ███ from being involved in the middle of the case or stressed because of the court litigation. The Court finds that it is proper to Order the Parties not to discuss the litigation with the minor child and not to allow the minor child to have access to documents which are litigation oriented.

In one motion, John had urged that the courts provide a mediator to investigate this horrible abuse. John wanted answers.

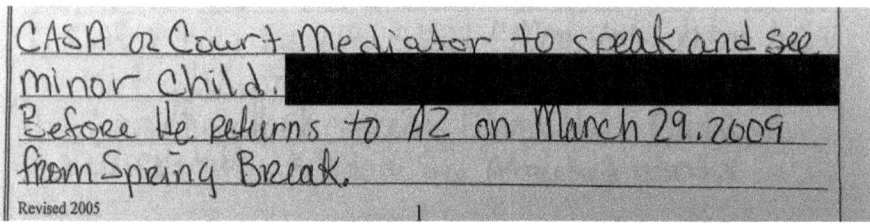

We waited for this fiasco to finally reach the court calendar for a hearing. It would be months before that would happen.

While sitting in the courtroom in September of 2009, the judge stated that he would not give John custody. John had failed to provide the courts with the proof needed for a custody change to be warranted. Judge Hardy had ordered that we attend mediation and assigned Phil Bushard to do an investigation of his own into the allegations that John had against myself and get an outsider view into Adam's mind. He was clear that depending on this report, he would make a ruling regarding custody. We wouldn't receive this report until April of 2010.

GOOD CAUSE APPEARING, the Court makes the following findings of fact, conclusions of law and enters the following Order:

FINDINGS OF FACT

1. The Court finds that Defendant, ███████████ has failed to meet his burden of proof to demonstrate that the minor child, █████████████████████ is not safe in the care of Plaintiff, Meghan ██████ The Court finds that Defendant has not met the requirements of Nevada law to demonstrate that a modification of primary physical custody is warranted and that Defendant failed to demonstrate that there has been a substantial change in circumstances affecting the welfare of the child or that the modification of custody serves the best interest of the child.

2. The Court finds that ██████ is thriving in school, is attending school on regular basis and his class work is acceptable. The Court finds that Plaintiff monitors the child's performance in school and has appropriate sanctions for missing homework. The Court finds that Plaintiff provides a safe and loving home for ██████

3. Defendant alleged that the child has been the victim of abuse. This Court does not find that ██████ has been the victim of child abuse. This Court finds that the allegations by

Defendant against Plaintiff and her Husband, ███████, are unfounded. Based upon the

allegations pled and the evidence at the hearing, the Court will not change custody of the

minor child. In light of the fact that Defendant lives in Nevada while the minor child and

Plaintiff live in Arizona, this Court finds that an evaluation to be conducted by Phil Bushard,

Director of the Family Court Mediation program for this Court would be of value for the

Court. This Court believes that after receipt of the report from Phil Bushard, to be completed

no later than March 1, 2010, and if warranted a supplemental custody review hearing will be

Ordered by the Court to be conducted in June, 2010.

As 2009 was wrapping up, I was even more frustrated with the courts. There was no finality. It seemed as if the courts were happy to stroke John's ego and in the end, encourage his filings of malicious motions. The courts provided this revolving door that allowed John and Jane to continue their attacks.

It was even more clear than ever that I would never get this to stop, the whole time a 10-year-old boy was suffering and battling within himself. I can't even begin to describe the heartbreaking moments that we, mother and son were going through. I maintained open communication with my son, but restricted information in his best interests. John and Jane were never concerned with how this was affecting Adam, despite the pleas from Adam.

4/13/09

Dear Mr. Starkey,

Having to write things in my journal relea bothers me. I just don't feel right. So just alow me to do something else pleace. I realy hate this. My live is bad eroph right now. So do i t pleas. I hate my life right now. Having to go to court is bad enoghf. No nine year old Should have to do that shold they? I cant focuse, sleep, or even talk with my dad about that Without getting heart burn.

95. 3105 - Ord Granting ...	22-Dec-2009	*Extra Text: ORDER GRANTING ORDER TO SHOW CAUSE - Transaction 1223518 - Approved By: NOREVIEW : 12-22-2009:14:38:10*
96. 4250 - Verification of ...	30-Nov-2009	*Extra Text: VERIFICATION OF PLAINTIFF: OPPOSITION TO MOTION FOR ORDER TO SHOW CAUSE*
97. 3860 - Request for Submission	25-Nov-2009	*Extra Text: DOCUMENT TITLE: MOTION TO SHOW CAUSE REGARDING CONTEMPT PARTY SUBMITTING: JOHN DOE DATE SUBMITTED: 11/25/09 SUBMITTED BY: N. DELADO DATE RECEIVED JUDGE OFFICE:*
100. 3795 - Reply...	25-Nov-2009	*Extra Text: REPLY TO RESPONSE TO MOTION JOHN DOE*
101. 2540 - Notice of Entry of Ord	17-Nov-2009	*Extra Text:*
102. 2645 - Opposition to Mtn ...	16-Nov-2009	*Extra Text: OPPOSITION TO MOTION FOR ORDER TO SHOW CAUSE*
105. 2700 - Ord After Hearing...	10-Nov-2009	*Extra Text: ORDER AFTER SEPTEMBER 25, 2009, HEARING - Transaction 1144989 - Approved By: NOREVIEW : 11-10-2009:13:38:06*
106. 2145 - Mtn Ord to Show Cause	04-Nov-2009	*Extra Text: MOTION FOR ORDER TO SHOW CAUSE REGARDING CONTEMPT*
108. 2610 - Notice ...	02-Nov-2009	*Extra Text: NOTICE OF SERVICE OF SCHOOL SCHEDULE UPON DEFENDANT*
109. 3860 - Request for Submission	26-Oct-2009	*Extra Text: DOCUMENT TITLE: OBJECTION TO PROPOSED ORDER PARTY SUBMITTING: JOHN DOE DATE SUBMITTED: 10/27/09 SUBMITTED BY: ASIMPSON DATE*

		RECEIVED JUDGE OFFICE:
110. 2630 - Objection to ...	26-Oct-2009	*Extra Text: OBJECTION TO PROPOSED ORDER*
112. 3860 - Request for Submission	21-Oct-2009	*Extra Text: DOCUMENT TITLE: ORDER AFTER HEARING DATE SUBMITTED: 10/21/09 SUBMITTED BY: JSHEETS DATE RECEIVED JUDGE OFFICE:*
115. 3174 - Ord re Family Mediation Prog	25-Sep-2009	*Extra Text: ORDER SETTING TELEPHONIC MEDIATION APPOINTMENT OCTOBER 20, 2009 @ 1:00 PM*
121. $1985 - **$Motion/Opposition Notice	08-Sep-2009	*Extra Text:*
122. 2645 - Opposition to Mtn ...	08-Sep-2009	*Extra Text:*
123. 3370 - Order ...	17-Jul-2009	*Extra Text: ORDER ADDRESSING EX PARTE MOTION - Transaction 904063 - Approved By: NOREVIEW : 07-17-2009:08:03:41*
124. 3370 - Order ...	17-Jun-2009	*Extra Text: ORDER ACKNOWLEDGING RECEIPT*
125. 3860 - Request for Submission	15-Jun-2009	*Extra Text: DOCUMENT TITLE: TO GRANT EMERGENCY CUSTODY OF MINOR CHILD PARTY SUBMITTING: JOHN DOE DATE SUBMITTED: 6/15/09 SUBMITTED BY: CPARSLEY DATE RECEIVED JUDGE OFFICE:*
128. 3860 - Request for Submission	12-Jun-2009	*Extra Text: DOCUMENT TITLE: FINANCIAL DISCLOSURE PARTY SUBMITTING: JOHN DOE DATE SUBMITTED: 06/12/09 SUBMITTED BY: JSHEETS DATE RECEIVED JUDGE OFFICE:*

129. 3370 - Order ...	29-May-2009	*Extra Text: ORDER DENYING MOTION FOR RECONSIDERATION; SETTING HEARING REGARDING CHILD SUPPORT; HOLDING REQUEST FOR APPOINTMENT OF CASA AND UNCOVERED MEDICAL EXPENSES IN ABEYANCE PENDING HEARING; DENYING PLAINTIFF'S REQUEST FOR SANCTIONS; HOLDING PLAINTIFF'S REQUEST FOR ATTORNEY'S FEES IN ABEYANCE; DIRECTING DEFENDANT TO MAINTAIN HEALTH INSURANCE FOR THE MINOR CHILD*
130. 3795 - Reply...	27-Apr-2009	*Extra Text: TO RESPONSE TO MOTION*
131. 3795 - Reply...	27-Apr-2009	*Extra Text: REPLY TO RESPONSE TO MOTION*
132. 3880 - Response...	27-Apr-2009	*Extra Text: RESPONSE TO MOTION*
134. 3860 - Request for Submission	27-Apr-2009	*Extra Text: DOCUMENT TITLE: MOTION TO CHANGE CUSTODY PARTY SUBMITTING: JOHN DOE DATE SUBMITTED: 04/27/09 SUBMITTED BY: JN DATE RECEIVED JUDGE OFFICE:*
137. 3860 - Request for Submission	27-Apr-2009	*Extra Text: DOCUMENT TITLE: REPLY TO RESPONSE TO MOTION OF EX PARTE PARTY SUBMITTING: JOHN DOE DATE SUBMITTED: 04/27/09 SUBMITTED BY: JN DATE RECEIVED JUDGE OFFICE:*
139. $1985 - **$Motion/Opposition Notice	16-Apr-2009	*Extra Text: MEGHAN A. BAILEY*

140. 2315 - Mtn to Dismiss ...	16-Apr-2009	*Extra Text: MOTION TO DISMISS ; MOTION TO STRIKE; OPPOSITION TO REQUEST FOR CASA OR COURT MEDIATOR MEGHAN A. BAILEY*
142. 3880 - Response...	08-Apr-2009	*Extra Text: TO MOTION*
143. 2490 - Motion ...	08-Apr-2009	*Extra Text:*
145. 4105 - Supplemental ...	30-Mar-2009	*Extra Text: SUPPLEMENT RE: OSC MEDICAL BILL ISSUE*
146. 2840 - Ord Denying ...	26-Mar-2009	*Extra Text: ORDER DENYING EX PARTE MOTION TO APPOINT CASA OR COURT MEDIATIOR; LEAVE TO RESUBMIT AS A NOTICED MOTION*
147. 3860 - Request for Submission	18-Mar-2009	*Extra Text: DOCUMENT TITLE: EMERGENCY MOTION REGARDING CHILDREN PARTY SUBMITTING: JOHN DOE DATE SUBMITTED: 03/18/09 SUBMITTED BY: JSHEETS DATE RECEIVED JUDGE OFFICE:*
148. 3370 - Order ...	09-Mar-2009	*Extra Text: ORDER DENYING MOTION FOR MODIFICATION OF CUSTODY; GRANTING PLAINTIFF'S MOTION FOR REVIEW OF CHILD SUPPORT; HOLDING REQUEST TO MAINTAIN HEALTH INSURANCE IN ABEYANCE; HOLDING REQUEST FOR PAYMENT OF UNCOVERED MEDICAL EXPENSES IN ABEYANCE*
149. 2645 - Opposition to Mtn ...	27-Feb-2009	*Extra Text: OPPOSITION TO MOTION TO CHANGE CUSTODY OF THE MINOR CHILD; MOTION FOR INCREASE IN CHILD SUPPORT AND 3 YEAR REVIEW*

150. 3860 - Request for Submission	27-Feb-2009	*Extra Text: DOCUMENT TITLE: MOTION FILED JANUARY 22, 2009 PARTY SUBMITTING: JOHN DOE DATE SUBMITTED: 02/27/09 SUBMITTED BY: JN DATE RECEIVED JUDGE OFFICE:*
154. $1985 - **$Motion/Opposition Notice	22-Jan-2009	*Extra Text:*
155. 2490 - Motion ...	22-Jan-2009	*Extra Text: JOHN DOE*

CHAPTER 8

2010

I had sought the help of counseling services in Arizona for Adam. After one phone call with John, Adam was crying so hard in his bedroom that his face had swollen up. It looked as if he had just had a horrible reaction to a shellfish allergy. This had to stop. I needed to get Adam some help, he needed relief from this. Sessions were held once a week in the home where it was requested that I participate. I was at a loss, I had no idea how to get this to stop, how to help Adam, or what more I could possibly do. John and Jane just continued with their attacks.

Adam would come home after visitation and be very emotional and nervous. He would tell me that his dad and Jane told him that he wouldn't be living with his mother much longer, that CPS would come take him away. You could see that Adam was being tortured inside, yet… no one would listen to me or him…

Child Protection Services

On March 25, 2010, my husband at the time and I received a visit from Child Support Services, investigating alleged physical abuse. I knew exactly where the report had originated from. We complied with the Case worker in her attempts to investigate. We also provided statements and information regarding John and his girlfriend. We were required to go in for drug testing because of the alleged report that I had been under the influence of drugs and alcohol.

I could not believe that this had gotten this far, that the animosity John felt for me was so severe that he would put his son at risk like this. The report given by John and his girlfriend is littered with outrageous and exaggerated accounts of false abuse in our home. In one statement, John admitted that he was not happy with my move to Arizona and at the time of this report wanted the child in his home.

John had implied that Ken and I were violent alcoholics with a history of domestic violence and abuse. He claimed that the now infamous year of 2008 was so horrific that Adam was thrown through a wall, had bruises and scars. John had claimed that I had locked Adam in his room for so long that he had to urinate on himself. They alleged neglect and stated that Adam had never been to the doctor and when he was last seen at the dentist, he had 5 cavities. The allegations were horrific to say the least. No wonder CPS showed up. John painted an abhorrent picture. I knew that they would interview Adam alone and I left it at that. John had claimed that Adam had been burned and beaten and there was a huge scar on his forehead.

Adam's face-to-face interview with CPSS Salas would shed some much-needed light on this matter. Finally, someone outside of this with no personal attachment would get a good look as to what was going on in this child's life.

ADAM'S INTERVIEW

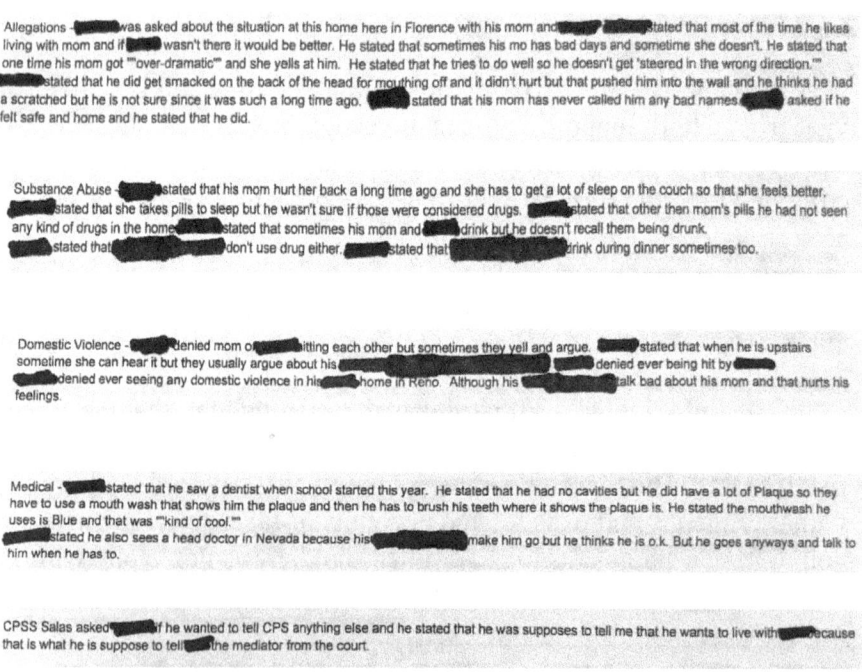

Allegations - ██████ was asked about the situation at this home here in Florence with his mom and ██████ ██████ stated that most of the time he likes living with mom and if ██████ wasn't there it would be better. He stated that sometimes his mo has bad days and sometime she doesn't. He stated that one time his mom got "'over-dramatic'" and she yells at him. He stated that he tries to do well so he doesn't get 'steered in the wrong direction.'" ██████ stated that he did get smacked on the back of the head for mouthing off and it didn't hurt but that pushed him into the wall and he thinks he had a scratched but he is not sure since it was such a long time ago. ██████ stated that his mom has never called him any bad names ██████ asked if he felt safe and home and he stated that he did.

Substance Abuse - ██████ stated that his mom hurt her back a long time ago and she has to get a lot of sleep on the couch so that she feels better. ██████ stated that she takes pills to sleep but he wasn't sure if those were considered drugs. ██████ stated that other than mom's pills he had not seen any kind of drugs in the home ██████ stated that sometimes his mom and ██████ drink but he doesn't recall them being drunk. ██████ stated that ██████ don't use drug either. ██████ stated that ██████ drink during dinner sometimes too.

Domestic Violence - ██████ denied mom o ██████ itting each other but sometimes they yell and argue. ██████ stated that when he is upstairs sometime she can hear it but they usually argue about his ██████ denied ever being hit by ██████ ██████ denied ever seeing any domestic violence in his ██████ home in Reno. Although his ██████ talk bad about his mom and that hurts his feelings.

Medical - ██████ stated that he saw a dentist when school started this year. He stated that he had no cavities but he did have a lot of Plaque so they have to use a mouth wash that shows him the plaque and then he has to brush his teeth where it shows the plaque is. He stated the mouthwash he uses is Blue and that was "'kind of cool.'" ██████ stated he also sees a head doctor in Nevada because his ██████ make him go but he thinks he is o.k. But he goes anyways and talk to him when he has to.

CPSS Salas asked ██████ f he wanted to tell CPS anything else and he stated that he was supposes to tell me that he wants to live with ██████ because that is what he is suppose to tell ██████ the mediator from the court.

Salas, the case worker for CPS provided in the records her findings on this report. Stating that there was no abuse and both my husband and I were more than capable of providing for Adam and the other children in the home. However, she went on to say that:

"It is apparent that they [John and his girlfriend Jane] have coached [Adam] in what he needs and should say to CPS with little regard for his emotional state"

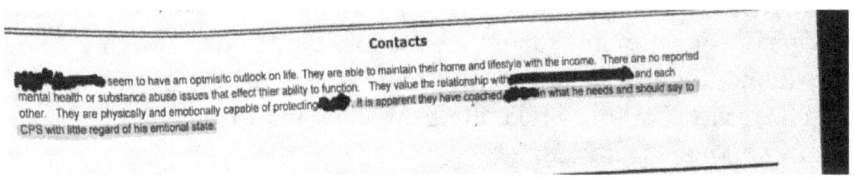

On July 28, 2010, I received a letter stating that the investigation of September 09, 2009 had been completed and that the report of child neglect had been found unsubstantiated and was now closed.

To say I was frustrated was an understatement. How could a person lie so much? Did he not care about his son? What this was doing to him? I realized early on that you cannot make someone be a parent, but a decent minded person would not go to these lengths to torment their ex. And do it all at the risk of harming their own child. We now had even more issues to deal with during our counseling sessions at home. John had now involved my daughter and put her at risk as well. Did either of my children deserve this? I don't believe they did.

I had done some digging around of my own, trying to understand John and Jane. I had found that in Jane's own previous divorce, actions like this were common place. She was as relentless then as she was now. In more ways than not, Jane's own Divorce case mirrored that of John and I's. I believed that Jane was pushing John to do this because she herself had lost custody of her own son. Nearly all the court documents filed by John were in her handwriting, no doubt she was just as much a part of this as John was, maybe even more so.

John stated that he was filing for full custody of the child and a hearing was set for September 25, 2009. It would seem that the sole purpose of this report was to show the court the alleged heinous attacks that were being committed in the home. Unfortunately, the process would take several months to complete. The judge dismissed the Motion to Change Custody.

In April 2010, we received the report from Phil Bushard. A lot was at stake with this report. I knew that neither John nor I would be squeaky clean in this report. How could we? Look at what we were doing to our son. I took this report as a chance to get a better and clearer look at this whole thing. What could I improve on? What did my son need from me?

Phil Bushard was very thorough in his investigation. He interviewed my mother, the school, the teachers, counselors, CPS agent, John, Jane, Ken and myself. It was painfully clear that this attack/defend cycle that had been going on through the courts needed to stop. One of us needed to be a parent and stop this. Phil Bushard had concluded that while John and Jane stressed that there was horrible abuse in my home, after interviewing school counselors as well as CPS, Adam was safe in my home.

FINAL COMMENTS

The dynamic of looking for negatives puts ▮▮▮▮ in a continued distress. Although ▮▮▮▮ is on many measures just fine with his mother, the youngster wants to live with his father. Its difficult to judge what comes first – the understandable desire of a youth who just would like to live with his dad, the continued efforts to 'catch' the other household with an allegation, or the conclusion of a kid that to get out of the middle I need to chose a side – and I chose dad.

This report is submitted without any recommendations regarding custody. If the matter is set for a hearing, please advise if any supplemental report and/or recommendations are required.

Phil Bushard

Phil Bushard

Judge Hardy had received the report and ruled that there be no changes in custody, Adam would continue to live with me.

ORDER

Upon review of the evaluation report provided by Phil Bushard, this Court

determines that no further proceedings are necessary.

IT IS SO ORDERED.

Dated: June **25**, 2010.

David A. Hardy
David A. Hardy
District Court Judge

John disagreed. He filed an Objection to Master's Recommendation. John had chosen to completely ignore the recommendations of Phil Bushard regarding stopping these litigations.

(Name of Master who signed the Recommendation)

Review of the Master's Recommendations is requested for the following reasons:

Do not believe that the Evaluation Report from Phil Bushard was entirely and fully Reviewed

Do not believe that the courts is taking the importance of the Childs well being seriously

There are evidences that the Child is stressed at Mothers home. Child is not able to express himself with out consequence of punishment for expressing how he feels.

The report for Phil Bushard, CPS. and Childrens Cabinet should be considered.

I had a hard time holding my tongue with this latest filing. I had already gone through CPS, counseling in the home, Phil Bushard, and yet despite them not finding ANY evidence what so ever of this alleged abuse, John and Jane continued to push. The real abuse was in their alienation, continued filings, and interrogation tactics with Adam. Even though they had gotten what they had asked for, i.e. A court mediator to investigate, the conclusions of these investigations would not collaborate with the horrible and vile picture they had been painting of me. The conclusions would not support their lies or intentions. John and Jane were unable to see past their vindictive nature to see what was happening to Adam. My attorney however, had to respond to this latest filing. In doing so, some very good points were made.

13	██████████ accused this Court of not taking ██████ 's well
14	being seriously. This is perhaps the lowest blow that hit in
15	this document. This Court has erred on the side of caution
16	throughout this litigation. This Court demanded that Ms. ██████
17	attend the hearing, at great expense, in person so that this
18	Court could review the credibility of the parties. This Court
19	demanded that Ms. ██████ demonstrate ongoing phone contact with
20	the father and child. This did not come at an easy expense as
21	telephone records had to be compiled, reduced to something
22	intelligible and presented to the Court. This Court ordered an
23	evaluation by Phil Bushard, even after stating that ██████████
24	had not met his burden of proof for a change in custody. ██████
25	██

██████████████████████████████████████ This Court asked that ██████ be allowed to step out of the middle and live his life as a child. In return, the latest motion was filed by ██

██████

██████████ knows this Court considered the unsubstantiated CPS report, the Children's Cabinet records that were admitted at the hearing and Phil Bushard's report. To state otherwise is belied by the record.

John and Jane both would not stop. Was their goal really to "help" Adam? This was clearly not the best way.

During one hearing, John had testified that the stress of all this litigation had caused him to have a heart attack. When asked whether John had an EKG or was admitted to a hospital by the judge, John became confused and even more defensive. He turned towards my mother, who had attended nearly every hearing, and tried to get her support. My mother quickly turned away and Jane lept up and had to add into the dramatization that this was so horrible. Jane was quickly scolded by the Bailiff to remain seated. I had always wondered, if this was so stressful for John and it was causing health problems, WHY was he continuing this? Why was he bombarding the courts with these frivolous motions?

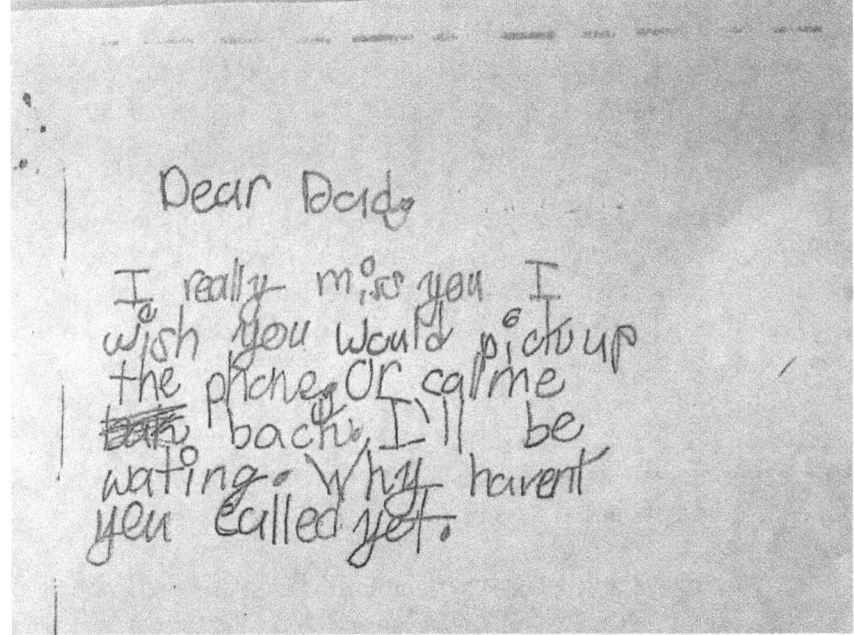

Child Support

In August of 2010, I decided to see what could be done as far as switching my child support case to the State of Arizona for Enforcement. I had no luck with Nevada enforcing the child support, and felt that there was a more personal connection with John and the case worker then.

I called Juddie Sayles, our then case worker on August 06, 2010 and left a message asking that she return my phone call. I did not hear back from her. On August 25, 2010, I placed another phone call to Juddie Sayles and left yet another message. I stated that I had questions regarding an issue with no actions being taken by their office to enforce the child support arrearages. I stated that if I did not receive a call back, I would be sending a certified letter stating that there had been no contact with her.

Shortly after making this phone call, I received a call from Juddie's supervisor. I spoke to her and told her that I wanted to transfer my child support case to the State of Arizona, and what did I need to do to complete this. I was shocked at the conversation between myself and this case worker. The Supervisor stated to me that:

"John was just in our office a few minutes ago and he stated that he wanted his child support reduced because he was only working 15-20 hours."

I explained to the supervisor that the order for the amount of child support was entered earlier in June. The supervisor acknowledged this fact and stated that there had already been a tax offset sent for the arrears, however, if John did not get a refund no money could be collected.

I explained to the supervisor that while I certainly understand that you cannot get blood from a turnip, this did not negate the fact that there were no previous tax offsets collected during the times when John was in arrears and did receive a refund.

The supervisor became sympathetic and stated that John continues to fall behind on his child support and thus is accruing more arrears, putting him in a difficult position.

Finally, after growing tired of the patty-cake game, I simply asked what it was that I needed to do in order to get this case transferred to Arizona. The supervisor stated:

"He [John] is here and has said that he does not want Arizona to enforce the order."

In so little words, I stated that I did not care, frankly… the child resides in Arizona with me, the custodial parent and their lack of enforcement and bias is the basis for this being done.

The supervisor replied:
"Well he is working on getting disability and would like to keep the case here in Nevada."

I explained again that I did not care, I wanted my case closed and I wanted it transferred to Arizona so they could begin enforcement. I explained to the supervisor that their failure in enforcing this child support case was grotesque and I did not appreciate her bias attitude towards the non-custodial parent.

The supervisor then stated that she could not guarantee that Nevada would be able to work with Arizona in the enforcement action. I hung up the phone, frustrated and felt the air slip out. I felt that this could not be right, how could a case worker within the child support enforcement division be so bias towards the non-custodial parent?

I began thinking that if this was happening to me, it had to be happening to others, both mothers and fathers. My suspicions regarding the bias in that office towards John was confirmed in that phone call. I wrote a lengthy letter to the Director of Child Support Enforcement and sent copies to the District Attorney as well.

In this letter, I detailed the reasons why I was frustrated. On June 15, 2010, the court entered its order that the John's arrears were set at $1, 662.81. While I understood that the economy was rough for every individual, and there may not be any monies to collect for these arrears if the non-custodial parent was not working. However, in 2009 John had received a refund in the amount of $705.00 for the 2008 tax year. On April 29, 2009, I received a letter from the District Attorney's Office stating that John's arrears were $660.19 as of March 31, 2009. The minimum amount of $500.00 in order to start a tax offset was met, making me question why his refund was not taken in order to pay off those arrears.

I received a call back a short time after their offices received the letter, some woman working in the Child Support Office simply stating that the case would be closed and enforcement through Arizona could begin. There was no response to the other questionable acts by their office stated in the letter, and I never received correspondence from the District Attorney's Office.

73. 2650 - Opposition to ...	08-Jul-2010	*Extra Text: OPPOSITION TO MOTION/OBJECTION TO MASTER'S RECOMMENDATION & NOTICE TO SET/MOTION TO STRIKE NOTICE TO SET*
74. 2540 - Notice of Entry of Ord	06-Jul-2010	*Extra Text:*
76. 2620 - Obj to Master's Recommendation	30-Jun-2010	*Extra Text:*
78. 3370 - Order ...	25-Jun-2010	*Extra Text: Transaction 1566001 - Approved By: NOREVIEW : 06-25-2010:19:18:01*
80. 3835 - Report...	20-Apr-2010	*Extra Text: Transaction 1438473 - Approved By: AZION : 04-20-2010:10:07:27*
81. 2540 - Notice of Entry of Ord	30-Mar-2010	*Extra Text:*
82. 2700 - Ord After Hearing...	29-Mar-2010	*Extra Text: ORDER AFTER HEARING - Transaction 1399916 - Approved By: NOREVIEW : 03-29-2010:11:47:20*
83. 1315 - ** Case Closed	29-Mar-2010	*Extra Text: ORDER AFTER HEARING*
87. 4105 - Supplemental ...	28-Jan-2010	*Extra Text: SUPPLEMENTAL OPPOSITION TO MOTION FOR ORDER TO SHOW CAUSE*
88. 3835 - Report...	25-Jan-2010	*Extra Text: Transaction 1278387 - Approved By: AZION : 01-25-2010:12:40:45*

CHAPTER 9
2011

On January 7, 2011, I received a knock on my door. I was home with my daughter. I answered the door and immediately recognized the badge. I was getting yet another visit from Child Protective Services. This time, the messenger was an older lady. When I opened the door and recognized why she was there, I couldn't help but say, *"Back again so soon? I'm not surprised."* She introduced herself and I opened my home up to her. We sat down at the dining table, where my daughter was engaged in her project.

The Agent said to me, *"Well, the reason why I am here is because we had received a report of missing underwear."* My jaw almost hit the floor, but I was too busy holding in laughter. I wanted to say a few choice words, something along the lines of, "Oh so this is what CPS does when it has its low points." But I refrained and was polite.

We discussed the missing underwear, and I informed the agent that two days ago, after Adam had returned from visiting with his father I noticed that Adam came back with only two pairs of underwear. I was shocked, since I packed 7 pairs. Adam stated that he would call Jane and ask her. When she answered, Adam asked *"Did I leave any underwear there? I only have two pairs in my backpack and my mom packed more than just two"*

I overheard Jane say, *"Does your mom want me to buy you some and send them down there?"* I immediately said *"No, I'll just go and buy some new ones."* The phone call ended. I explained to the Agent that I knew where this report came from. She of course could not confirm or deny my assumptions, that is her job. We moved onto another topic, a "voo doo" bag. The report claimed that Adam was prescribed anti-psychotics and instead of giving Adam his medication, I had provided Adam some sort of "voo doo" bag.

I explained to the Agent that I did in fact give Adam a small leather bag, however it was not "voo doo", it contained Lavender, Sage, and Sweetgrass. Herbs commonly used as a calming effect. I stated that during counseling, the Nurse Practitioner stated that I could give Adam a Benadryl instead of the medication that she would prescribe. I was too worried about having another child in the world on medication that I chose to do the Benadryl and herbs. These had so far helped Adam with his anxiety.

As I walked away to take some copies for the Agent, she interviewed my youngest daughter. I came back and my daughter was sitting on the Agent's lap, talking about everything under the sun that was important to any 4-year-old. I sat back down and told the Agent that I couldn't believe that they would have to investigate an issue regarding "missing underwear" and a supposed "voodoo bag". She agreed that it was a ridiculous claim, but that she needed to do her job as well. I thanked her for coming by and walked her to the door.

With her gone, I looked at my daughter and decided I had had enough. This was crossing the line in this whole vicious battle. To put an innocent child that has absolutely nothing to do with the custody issue regarding Adam was appalling. I would do just as I had done before and get those records once this was closed.

During this investigation, Adam was interviewed as well at his school. It was painfully obvious that the grotesque picture that John and Jane tried to prove true was just not possible.

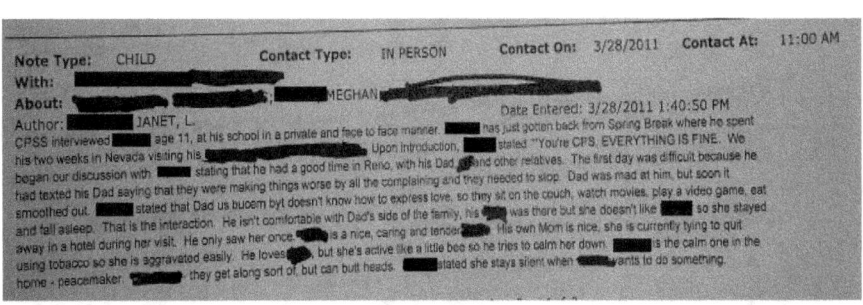

Adam expressed his wish that this would end.

It wasn't too long before the case was found unsubstantiated.

In the Summary of Current Report Allegations, it was reported that Adam was forced to wake up every morning to take care of his sister, and that I was often impaired from drinking and taking prescribed pain medication. Also noted was a history of domestic violence.

As I dove deeper and deeper into the records, I could feel my blood start to boil. This wasn't just about missing underwear or a "voo doo bag" this was about John and his girlfriend's hatred towards my husband and me. There were several calls made to the CPS Agent by John and his girlfriend Jane.

On February 2, 2011, there was a phone call made by John stating:

"Was quite insistent that Adam is living in an unsafe home and severely mistreated. CPSS Agent stated that no safety issues have been found. He then began to cry and almost yelled that "he" was concerned for "his" son and didn't want any harm to come to him. CPS isn't taking him seriously."

On February 10, 2011, another phone call was made, stating:

"CPS should take their reports seriously and Meghan is harassing "him" through texts. CPSS Agent stated there were no safety issues found in the home. John interrupted and stated to just disregard this call because "he" is just wasting our time".

On April 4, 2011, there was a phone call made by John stating:

"There is a "full-fledged Federal Investigation" going that found "he" should be the Primary Custodian. He has CPS in Nevada involved and the "Children's Cabinet" where Adam stated he was burned and beaten which left a big scar on his forehead. He stated he would send copies of the court reports to CPSS Bennett but Nevada refused to give up the paperwork to the State of Arizona."

In the assessment notes from the Agent, it is stated that

"Jane displays a need to control the issues of how unhappy Adam is, without question and persists on making accusations of abuse. Phone interview with bio Dad, revealing extraneous allegations which have been disproven previously. Family into dramatizing issues of custody and attention."

"Adam has communicated that he is not unhappy, is not maltreated, and is not in any danger, yet [John] persists on making accusations of abuse."

Despite having CPS in the home, a year earlier and having these absurd allegations disproven, John and Jane were relentless in their pursuit of destroying the relationship between my son and me. He would not stop, he could not be reasoned with, and he did not care who he was hurting in his personal vendetta.

I started to receive phone calls and magazine subscriptions that were not in the norm. I receive several calls from collectors looking for John's mother, a life insurance company wanting to give a quote stating that Adam had requested one. After some investigating on my part, it was found that John's own e mail address was used for the magazine subscriptions and countless other forms of harassment.

My attorney attempted to strike some common sense into John's brain after an officer was called to our home to check and make sure there were no new bruises on Adam.

Re: police visit

Dear ███

    I have been advised that the police came out to visit with ███ I will be requesting the police reports and reviewing the reason that the police were sent to the house. Needless to say, I am very frustrated that you continue to involve your child in courtroom drama and antics of this type. My understanding is that there was, and is, absolutely nothing wrong with ███ This type of act harms ███ in that he is continually torn between his home, his mother, his stepfather and his father. It is cruel on your part to generate such emotional abuse.

    I hope that you have some good reason or some good faith belief that you needed to take such an action. If your motivations were not in the clear, you may anticipate fall out from the continued harassment of my client. Perhaps the next time you would like to send the police you would actually call Meghan, ask her to put ███ on the phone and get some facts to deal with rather than placing ███ in the role of some victim. By the way, ███ is not a victim of abuse at the ███ residence. I am concerned that he is emotionally abused by your continued desire to place him into litigation as if he was a commodity of some type. The harm you are doing is to your own son. Please take time to investigate before reacting in this way.

Adam confronted his Dad one time that I am aware of. He also confronted Jane who seemed to be the main pusher in doing these things and also serving as John's own personal lawyer at times. In a series of text messages thing became a bit more clear.

------ SMS Text ------
From: ███████
Received: Jan 22, 2011 7:00 PM
Subject: FWD: how are you.

███████ FWD: how are you. wish you would talk to us. i understand that your pretty mad with dad.

------ SMS Text ------
From: ███████
Received: Jan 22, 2011 6:57 PM
Subject: FWD: yah did he get my message.

███████ FWD: yah did he get my message.

------ SMS Text ------
From: ███████
Received: Jan 22, 2011 7:01 PM
Subject: FWD: when?

███████ FWD: when? i thinl his phone is in room and he has been outside working on fence so reese will quite taking off.

------ SMS Text ------
From: ███████
Received: Jan 22, 2011 6:58 PM
Subject: FWD: thurs day night

███████ FWD: thurs day night

------ SMS Text ------
From: ███████
Received: Jan 22, 2011 7:01 PM
Subject: FWD: oh i dont know i will ask...

███████ FWD: oh i dont know i will ask him.

```
------ SMS Text ------
From: ████████
Received: Jan 22, 2011 6:59 PM
Subject: FWD: well what i  said was that if...

████████        FWD: well what i  said was that if  you guys dont quit fileing cps reports and
court papers just to get back at my mom ,its
hurting me than im not going to accept him as my father.   its really stupid
that you filed a report over underwere. i mean does ████deserve  getting tooken away from
mom. its kinda hard to not worry about cps when they come and talk to mom. and then they have
to come to my school and talk to me.

------ SMS Text ------
From: ████
Received: Jan 22, 2011 7:02 PM
Subject: FWD: hunter i can not beleive that...

████████        FWD: ████i can not beleive that you feel that way about your dad. we have
done nothing to you but try to protect you by what you have said to us. what are we supose to
think about the things

------ SMS Text ------
From: ████
Received: Jan 22, 2011 7:03 PM
Subject: FWD: that you have told us.

████████        FWD: that you have told us. your dad and i love you very much and have done
everything to keep you out of the middle as we talked about this when you were here at
christmas. dad never want to see you hurting. we have backed off. ████will always be your
dad no matter what...
I hope that you can see that we love you very much and dad feeling are very
hurt also. I hope that you come at spring break.

------ SMS Text ------
From: ████████
Received: Jan 22, 2011 7:10 PM
Subject: FWD: no you  guys havent friken...

████████        FWD: no you  guys havent friken back backed off. im sick of
your  bs  you guys .    i had a sever fucking anxiety attack on thurs.
because of this  shit . i had to call my counsler at 8 and i was hypervenalating.  you guys
havent even tried to fucking protect me your in
thre middle████and i know it.  you've hurt me so bad .    IVE HAD ENOUGH
OF YOUR BULLSHIT !!!!!!!!!!!!
```

```
From: ████████
Received: Jan 22, 2011 7:18 PM
Subject: FWD: and yes im coming for spring...

████████  FWD: and yes im coming for spring break  if you by the ticket. mom has no
choice i really dont want to.

------ SMS Text ------
From: ████████
Received: Jan 22, 2011 7:40 PM
Subject: FWD: what do you mean?

████████  FWD: what do you mean? we always but your ticket. we also are moving in next
week we got a house out by other house. 4bedroom 3 bath your room has bathoom in it.... well
i love you very much and miss you lots hunter
```

I was shocked for a few reasons, my son's use of the "F" word, him not really wanting to go up there, and how calm Jane was after receiving a pretty big lashing from Adam. Obviously, he was upset and was pleading with them to stop. Instead, a bedroom with its own bath was apparently more important. Would ANYONE really be able to get through to these people?

I had thought long and hard about the decision I was about to make when I walked into that courtroom. I knew that there was no reason for me to defend myself again for John's false allegations. It was obvious, through all these years and all the pleadings for someone to recognize what was happening to my son, I needed to stop being complacent and do something. I could not depend on the courts. The courts had failed every time and my faith in the justice system was lost completely.

I pondered the best ways for Adam to get out of the middle of this nightmare. So that someday he could actually live a normal life. I knew that as long as he was with me, John would never stop with his relentless litigation. I felt my heart being ripped out of my chest. Not one person in this terrible saga heard the pleas. But they were more than willing to entertain John and his grotesque actions. I watched my son suffer in so many heartbreaking ways for 17 years. I couldn't allow this to happen any longer.

Adam had been saying that he wanted to live with his father. But, the only way that I could keep my son away from the litigation nightmare and being in the middle was if I took John's ability to file any more litigation away. There was only one way to do that. I knew that if custody had just been switched and I was granted visitation, John would continue to file motion after motion. It was clear that he was absolutely determined to get me out of Adam's life.

I spoke with my attorney just before the hearing and told her my plan. She was not happy about it, but could not deny that it was the only possible solution. To try and save my son's life and give him the chance to grow up halfway normal and eliminate John's ability to continue this destructive path... I needed to sign over custody and petition to terminate my parental rights.

57 | P a g e

However, I did not want John to be able to eliminate my whole family out of Adam's life. I wanted to make sure that there was a way where Adam could still contact me if he wanted. I wanted to make sure that his Grandparents could still be a part of his life, I knew I would miss out on a lot, but I didn't think that they needed to suffer the same fate. If John was to have custody of Adam, he would have to give my parents Grandparents Rights.

I sat down with Adam and explained to him what had happened at the hearing and what my decision was. Adam cried and said that he did want to live with his dad, but not this way. I cried as well, and I tried to explain to Adam why this was necessary. Inside my heart was being ripped in half, I could do the only thing that was left to do… Pray. I prayed that my son would always know that I loved him and it is because of that love that I had to make this decision. I could see that all pleas for help were in vain and no one would be able to stop this…. Except for me. I had to make the ultimate sacrifice, a very disheartening decision to let my son go.

"Peace demands the most heroic labor and the most difficult sacrifice. It demands greater heroism than war. It demands greater fidelity to the truth and a much more perfect purity of conscience."
— Thomas Merton

December 2, 2011

My daughter was screaming for her brother not to leave from the backseat of my mother's car, she was uncontrollable and hysterical. As I tried to keep my own emotions in check, I kissed my son on the lips and told him that I would always love him. To remember only the good between this family and him. He walked towards John's car and I could see the smug look on John's face in the street lighting. I hated him… I hated him in a way that once you let that darkness in, it never leaves. I climbed back into my mother's car and we left. That would be the last time I saw my son until October 2014 and the last time a little sister saw her brother.

John had finally broken me… and I would never be the same again.

55. 3242 - Ord Setting Hearing	16-Sep-2011	*Extra Text: Transaction 2475506 - Approved By: NOREVIEW : 09-16-2011:16:06:40*
57. 1740 - Financial Declaration ...	14-Sep-2011	*Extra Text: FINANCIAL DISCLOSURE FORM - MEGHAN BAILEY*
58. 3860 - Request for Submission	22-Aug-2011	*Extra Text: DOCUMENT TITLE: MOTION FOR ORDER TO SHOW CAUSE (PAPER ORDER PROVIDED). DATE SUBMITTED: AUG. 22, 2011 SUBMITTED BY: TWHITE DATE RECEIVED JUDGE OFFICE:*
59. 3795 - Reply...	22-Aug-2011	*Extra Text: REPLY TO MOTION FOR ORDER TO SHOW CAUSE*
60. 2645 - Opposition to Mtn ...	16-Aug-2011	*Extra Text: OPPOSITION TO MOTION FOR ORDER TO APPEAR AND SHOW CAUSE - Transaction 2409526 - Approved By: AZION : 08-16-2011:09:29:16*
63. 1325 - ** Case Reopened	02-Aug-2011	*Extra Text:*
64. 3860 - Request for Submission	02-Aug-2011	*Extra Text: REPLY TO OPPOSITION TO MOTION FOR ORDER TO APPEAR AND SHOW CAUSE - Transaction 2381948 - Approved By: AZION : 08-02-2011:10:47:41 DOCUMENT TITLE: REPLY TO OPPOSITION TO MOTION FOR ORDER TO APPEAR AND SHOW CAUSE PARTY SUBMITTING: CARL HART ESQ DATE SUBMITTED: 08-02-11 SUBMITTED BY: AZION DATE RECEIVED JUDGE OFFICE:*
66. 3790 - Reply to/in Opposition	01-Aug-2011	*Extra Text: REPLY TO OPPOSITION TO MOTION FOR ORDER TO APPEAR AND SHOW CAUSE - Transaction 2381112 - Approved By: AZION : 08-02-2011:08:18:08*
67. 2645 - Opposition to Mtn ...	26-Jul-2011	*Extra Text: OPPOSITION TO MOTION FOR ORDER TO SHOW CAUSE*
68. 2145 -	26-	*Extra Text:*

Mtn Ord to Show Cause	Jul-2011	
70. 2145 - Mtn Ord to Show Cause	19-Jul-2011	*Extra Text: MOTION FOR ORDER TO APPEAR AND SHOW CAUSE - Transaction 2355110 - Approved By: AZION : 07-19-2011:14:48:47*
72. 2520 - Notice of Appearance	14-Jul-2011	*Extra Text: C. WILLIAM HART ESQ – JOHN DOE - Transaction 2347356 - Approved By: AZION : 07-15-2011:08:02:24*

CHAPTER 10

2012

STIPULATION AND ORDER RE: MODIFICATION OF CHILD CUSTODY, VISITATION, CHILD SUPPORT & INSURANCE FOR MINOR CHILD:

IT IS HEREBY STIPULATED AS FOLLOWS:

1.   **Custody.**   That actual physical custody of the minor child the subject of this marriage, to wit: : ▮▮▮▮▮▮▮▮▮▮▮▮ shall be changed and established with▮▮▮ The parties shall retain Joint Legal Custody of▮▮▮. ▮▮▮▮shall relocate to the Reno area to live with▮▮▮

   c. Meghan shall be ordered to pay child support in the amount of $100.00 per month, due and payable on the first day of each month. Until such time as the child support arrearage owed by▮▮▮to Meghan are satisfied in full, ~~Meghan~~ shall keep an accounting demonstrating the reduction of the outstanding arrearage and shall not deliver payment in monies to▮▮▮ After such time as the termination of parental rights is entered by the Court, the child support

3

obligation shall cease. If the Court fails to terminate the parental rights of Meghan, then once the child support arrearage is satisfied in full, Meghan shall pay child support in the amount of $100.00 per month by mailing said payment to▮▮▮latest address. ▮▮▮shall keep Meghan advised of his current residential address. All payments will be through Washoe County.

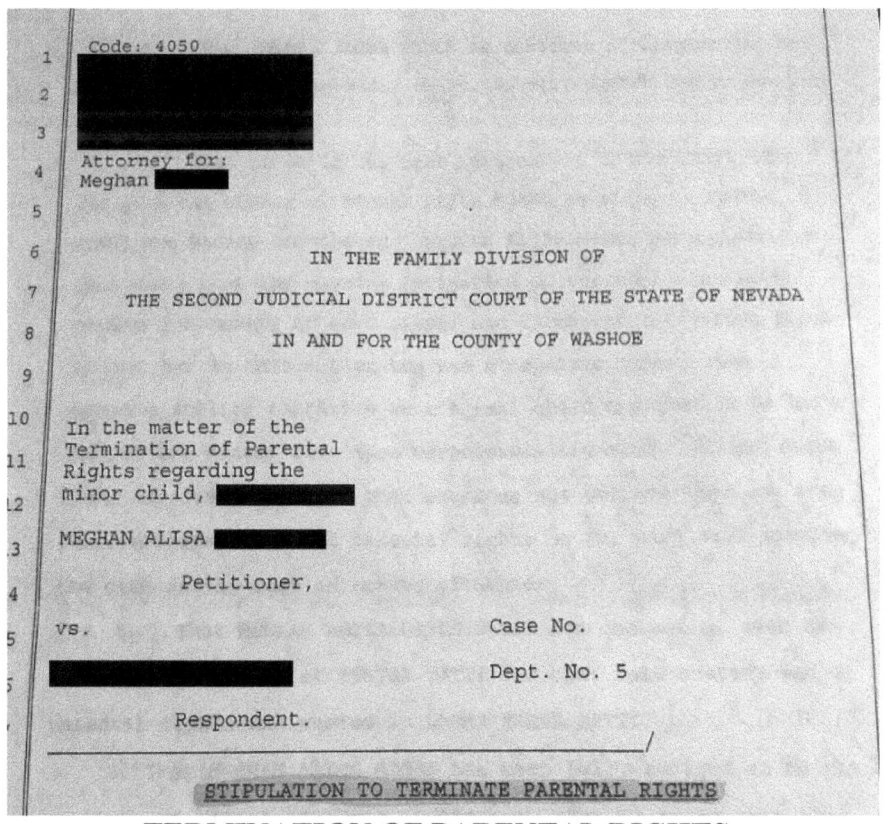

Code: 4050

Attorney for:
Meghan ▮▮▮

IN THE FAMILY DIVISION OF

THE SECOND JUDICIAL DISTRICT COURT OF THE STATE OF NEVADA

IN AND FOR THE COUNTY OF WASHOE

In the matter of the
Termination of Parental
Rights regarding the
minor child, ▮▮▮

MEGHAN ALISA ▮▮▮

     Petitioner,

vs.   Case No.

▮▮▮   Dept. No. 5

     Respondent.

STIPULATION TO TERMINATE PARENTAL RIGHTS

TERMINATION OF PARENTAL RIGHTS

We submitted our Stipulation to Terminate Parental Rights and had our hearing. I vaguely remember the attorney for John coming up to my attorney with a very solemn look on his face. He said, *"I didn't want it to end like this."*

I forgive his naivety on the case, he had not been a part of this case for long at all. He didn't know John's previous behavior in previous hearings. As the judge proceeded with the hearing, she asked if John was on any State aid. John seemed confused and the judge repeated her question. John spoke up *"Well, I get free money from the government, is that what you mean?"*

His attorney hung his head and apologized to the judge and to my attorney. He "didn't know". Apparently, John was less than truthful to his own attorney. The judge apologized and said that she could not grant the termination of rights because of this. Because

John has been receiving State aid, legally she could not voluntarily terminate my rights. My heart sunk. I wasn't relieved, how could I be? Now, there was no stopping John and his vexatious litigations. I would spend the better part of 2012 and 2013 treading very carefully. I did not want John to have any excuse to file more motions and hurl Adam right back in the middle of this mess. For now, I would play it out.

Subject: my new e mail
From:
Date: 4/16/2012 7:41 PM
To: Grandma
"Meghan

he mom and g-ma its me i got a new email. keep this for your adresses because this is the only one i will have. youll get another email later love ya bye

43. 3980 - Stip and Order... 20-Sep-2012 *Extra Text: RE: MODIFICATION OF CHILD CUSTODY, VISITATION, CHILD SUPPORT, AND INSURANCE FOR MINOR CHILD - Transaction 3228718 - Approved By: NOREVIEW : 09-20-2012:10:30:01*

CHAPTER 11

2013

Adam and I had emailed each other several times. We continued to talk when he was at his Grandmother's. The only real way we could have a decent conversation. I knew that I would not be able to afford to come see him and this was detrimental to our relationship. It was crucial that we keep in contact. Adam had said several times during our conversations that he just didn't feel like he could talk to me in front of John or Jane. The interrogation that followed after we hung up was too much for him to handle. He had said that he wasn't allowed to say "nice" things about me, if he did, they would always try to turn it into something more negative. Adam would call me while he was on the bus to school, but that did not last long as soon as he got home John and Jane would check the phone. Adam and I were never able to talk to each other in private.

Subject: hi
From: █████████████████████████
Date: 1/30/2013 8:31 PM
To: "Meghan █████████████████████████

Hey mom how are you?
I heard that you weren't able to use your phone, but that's OK I understand.
So what's been happening with u and ███ and ███?
How's Diesel and how's Shadow?
You been ghost hunting lately?
What is ███ learning in school?
I got a school project on the roaring 20's doesn't that sound like fun?
I also got a 3.8 which is an (A) on my math final that was 2 weeks ago.
guess what my (A.R.) level is the highest it can go which is college level; woooohoooo.
guess what I got lambs again, I might actually cry this time when I have to get rid of them.
I got the good lamb this year.
he's so adorable.
I've got so many friends this year its unbelievable, I'm soooooo happy. I want to jump for joy.
one of my friends named ███ is the funniest person I've ever met.
Heck, she even surpasses Efunk.
Then my LADY friend ███ is like the most realistic of the bunch.
Then there's ███ she's like the girly girl and the rainbows, sunshine, glitter, and unicorns type of girl. she's hilarious.
Then there's ██████ now he is the smart one, and he's very funny.
I also know this girl named ███ she's the quirky type.
I also love the telescope I got for Christmas.
my teachers also ask for me on tech problems isn't that cool.

Talk to you later, love you

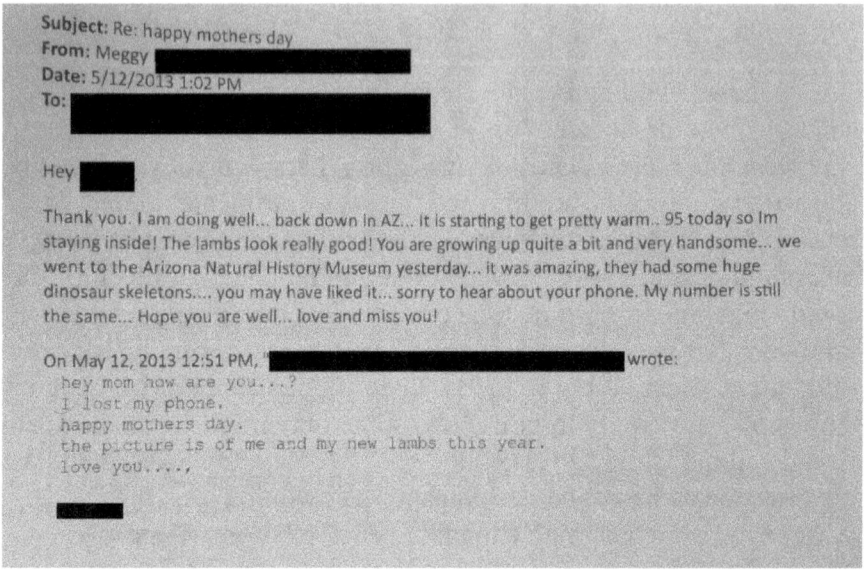

Subject: Re: happy mothers day
From: Meggy ██████████████
Date: 5/12/2013 1:02 PM
To: ████████████████████

Hey ████

Thank you. I am doing well... back down in AZ... it is starting to get pretty warm.. 95 today so Im staying inside! The lambs look really good! You are growing up quite a bit and very handsome... we went to the Arizona Natural History Museum yesterday... it was amazing, they had some huge dinosaur skeletons.... you may have liked it... sorry to hear about your phone. My number is still the same... Hope you are well... love and miss you!

On May 12, 2013 12:51 PM, ████████████████████ wrote:
hey mom how are you...?
I lost my phone.
happy mothers day.
the picture is of me and my new lambs this year.
love you....,

████████

Child Support

One of the issues that has really caused me to question the moral standards involved with the Child Support Office came to a head in 2013. After the order was signed and I felt that finally some relief could be gained from the barrage of attacks, I realized that I had once again let my guard down. The walls were just beginning to recede after the custody was settled.

My husband at the time and I had to file for our 2012 taxes. When we received our tax return, I noticed that the amount was not what we had expected. It was $600.00 short. I called the Financial Management Services number to find out what exactly was taken out, where it went, and more importantly why. There was one offset listed under myself, as I listened to the robotic voice tell me, I could feel the rage build inside. I'm almost certain that if I had looked in the mirror at this time, my face would have been 16 shades of red. The voice said:

"An offset was collected in the amount of $600.00, for information about this offset, please contact the party at (775) 789-7100."

I immediately recognized the number and called my attorney right away. As per the court order, and the letter sent by my attorney, it was crystal clear that the Child Support Enforcement office was in violation of a court order. Frankly, I was pissed.

I waited a few days for some word from my attorney regarding this, I decided that I would contact the Child Support Enforcement office myself and see what I could dig up on this. After waiting on hold for 1 hour and 15 minutes, I finally was able to speak with someone. Brittany came on the line and I told her the reason why I was calling. First, I wanted to confirm that they had received the order dated September 20, 2012. Brittany confirmed this, but became lost when I explained what the order stated, she kept telling me that I was in arrears of $650.00. I explained that this couldn't be possible because of what the order states. When questioned about John's arrears, she stated that she couldn't bring up that information because the case status was closed.

I requested that a full audit be completed on both cases, John's and my own. I wanted to know where the arrears had gone. I certainly had not received any monies owed, in fact I had spent the last two years with zero payments, while John's arrears continued to rise.

After receiving a response from my attorney, my anger went through the roof. When my attorney spoke with "Sherry", it was noted that the reason why Nevada is collecting payments from me was because John was on welfare.

I am not proud to admit that I too have had my hand forced to gain assistance from welfare, we do what we have to do in order to survive. I found this response from Sherry both frustrating and idiotic.

For 2 years while Adam was residing with me in Arizona, we were on government assistance, and for those two years not once did I ever receive a payment from John. During this time, Arizona was enforcing the court order for child support. There had been several attempts to collect and even enter interstate actions against John. Sadly, Arizona still had to deal with the absurd nature of the Washoe

County District Attorney's. It was realized in 2011 that Arizona would be unable to enforce any actions against John, the response from Nevada was that they had received a request to modify and were waiting on a court order. It would be 11 months before the child support office would receive the order stating that custody had been changed.

During those 11 months, Nevada refused to enforce Arizona's requests to collect. The order for custody was entered and accepted by the courts on September 20, 2012 by December I had received a notice for Tax Offset in the amount of $200.00. It was shocking to both my attorney and me that Nevada was so quick to collect against me when for many years, they refused to collect on John or investigate.

In March of 2013, John's arrears stood at $6,914.23.

CHAPTER 12

2014

The year 2014 turned out to be a trying year for our family. Adam and I had been talking on and off during the year. Many times, we would talk while he was with his grandparents or when John and Jane were not home. Adam had expressed several times that his phone conversations were monitored and after every call he would be interrogated in some way. Adam and I had decided that it would be best if we kept the contact limited so that he would not become so stressed with John and Jane's overwhelming paranoia.

On Mother's Day, I was shocked to not receive a text message from Adam wishing me a Happy Mother's Day. He never missed a chance to tell me that he loved me. I had contacted my mother and asked if she had heard from him, she hadn't. Things became busy and I figured that Adam would call me or text me when he could.

In July, Adam had gone to his grandparents for visitation. I spoke with Adam over the phone. He told me that he had been admitted into West Hills Hospital because of his attempt at suicide. I was unaware that he was having emotional issues so severe that this would have been an option. I asked Adam why his father did not notify me of this, Adam stated to me that his dad told my mother and figured that she would inform me. This is apparent here that John was not interested in co-parenting, and had no sense of compassion.

As it turns out, the Washoe County Sheriff's Department was called to respond to John's residence. Adam was admitted into West Hills on May 02, 2014. Adam had spent 10 days in West Hills under supervision. This was why I had not heard from him on Mother's Day. Adam's grandmother was told a week after Adam had been released from West Hills.

Had I known that my son was doing so poorly, I would have acted. John of course, conveniently chose not to inform me. There was never any indication that Adam's mental state was being disrupted by him and I talking. Adam knew that after every phone call or email, he would be questioned as to what him and I talked about. My mother would pick Adam up in Reno and bring him back up to Spring Creek, Nevada for a week or two at a time. She never once had an issue with Adam. He never seemed fearful and would be eager to talk to me on the phone. Knowing that Grandma's house was more of a safe zone than anything, there was no pressure.

In August, I had made a decision to move up to Spring Creek, Nevada. I found myself again living in my parent's home with a young child. Marriage number 2 did not work out as planned. After not being able to visit my son during the past 2 years, I wanted to see him. I was closer, money was available, and the timing was right. In September, I sent an email to John letting him know that I was giving my 24-hour notice to have my visitation with my son. I drove to Reno with my daughter and my mother. We had been planning a visit with my brother for a while.

I had not been able to see much of my family while I was living in Arizona. My son had not seen my daughter in a long time. This visitation was important for both of my children. I received an email from John stating that he was not going to allow this visitation. I replied back and stated that I would meet him at the GSR the next morning to see Adam and would drop him off later that day. I was simply asking for 7 hours. The next morning, I arrived at GSR and waited for John to bring Adam, after waiting over an hour, I texted John. He refused my visitation. I contacted the Washoe County Sheriff's Department and waited another hour for a deputy to arrive. He reviewed the custody papers and explained that there was nothing he could do. He said the papers were missing a clause in them that prevented him from helping to facilitate my visitation.

The papers needed to have in there that if the other party denies the other of their visitation or is in violation of this order, the courts order law enforcement to take that party into custody. The current disclaimer would not suffice for the Deputy to take action. Earlier that morning I had noticed that John had filed a document with the courts the day that he had received notice from me. I did not know what this document was, but I was highly upset. I immediately notified my attorney of the refusal of visitation and this latest filing in the courts.

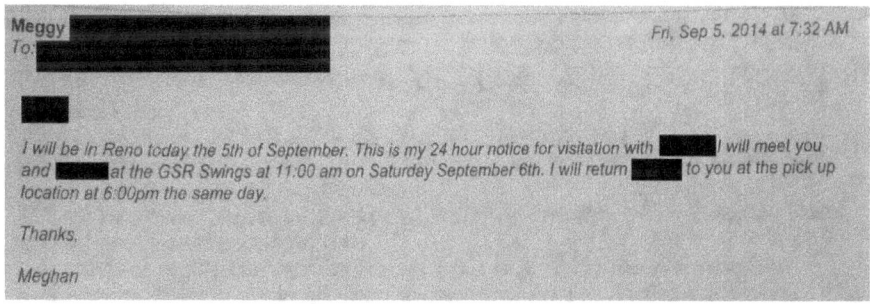

Meggy ▮▮▮▮▮▮▮▮▮▮▮▮▮▮▮▮▮   Fri, Sep 5, 2014 at 7:32 AM
To: ▮▮▮▮▮▮▮▮▮▮▮▮▮▮▮▮

▮▮▮

I will be in Reno today the 5th of September. This is my 24 hour notice for visitation with ▮▮▮ I will meet you and ▮▮▮ at the GSR Swings at 11:00 am on Saturday September 6th. I will return ▮▮▮ to you at the pick up location at 6:00pm the same day.

Thanks,

Meghan

Visitation

▮▮▮▮▮▮▮▮▮▮▮▮▮▮▮▮   Fri, Sep 5, 2014 at 4:42 PM
To: Meggy ▮▮▮▮▮▮▮▮▮▮

Meghan,
This is to inform you that I will NOT be allowing any visitation at this time.
You have not seen ▮▮▮ in almost 3 years. For Me to just drop ▮▮▮ off with you after all this time is out of the question and not recommended.
You and Your Parents do not want to understand ▮▮▮ mental situation and I will not allow ▮▮▮ to be subjected to more emotional distress.
See court documentation that Mediation was to be done with in 90 days after your request for termination of your rights was denied. Before any Visitation takes place, Mediation needs to be started.
Thank you

▮▮▮

[Quoted text hidden]

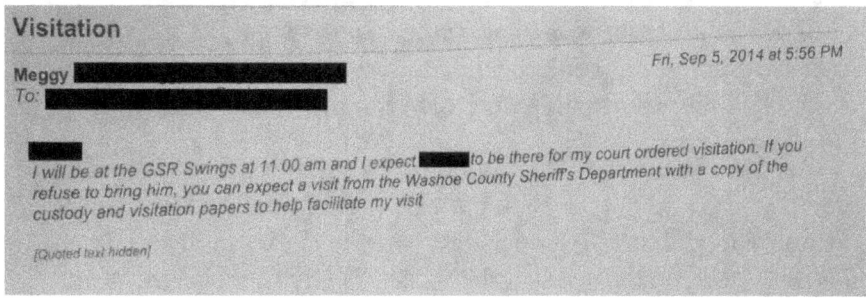

Visitation

Meggy ▮▮▮▮▮▮▮▮▮▮▮▮▮   Fri, Sep 5, 2014 at 5:56 PM
To: ▮▮▮▮▮▮▮▮▮▮▮▮▮▮

▮▮▮

I will be at the GSR Swings at 11:00 am and I expect ▮▮▮ to be there for my court ordered visitation. If you refuse to bring him, you can expect a visit from the Washoe County Sheriff's Department with a copy of the custody and visitation papers to help facilitate my visit

[Quoted text hidden]

It was at this time that I started to question what was going on and how truthful Adam was being, with both John and myself. I decided to get the records from West Hills to get to the bottom of this. Those records then led me to Alliance Family Services in Reno, Nevada where Adam was being seen by a Dr. Edward Lynam. After receiving those records and getting a very clear picture of who and what I was dealing with, my heart shattered. I had been played for a fool by my own child. John, Jane and Adam were all included in these counseling sessions. John was the major contributor however, Adam had his own stories to tell. I immediately sent this Dr. Lynam all of Adam's previous mental health records from counselors in Arizona. Surely, he would be able to see the contradictions in stories and how Adam would play one role with me and another with John.

Dr. Lynam would not though. Even after being given these records, he could not go back on his word. It was Dr. Lynam who recommended that I be given supervised visitation. I decided that this was ludicrous, if I was to be forced to have supervised visitation with my son, I wanted it to be with his counselors. I would set up a day where I would travel from Elko, Nevada to Reno, Nevada and attend a counseling session with Adam. If there were any "real" issues, Adam would surely be comfortable enough to discuss them there.

Right away, John was insistent that him and Jane be allowed in these sessions. He did not want me to be alone with the counselors. I refused, as much animosity that exists between John and I, it would not be conducive to Adam's health. I ended up seeing Adam a few times under these circumstances.

I wanted to put a face to this "monster" that they described, I wanted Adam's counselors to get an idea of who they were talking about. In the end, I gave up with the supervised visitations. Accepting something like that was like admitting that there may be "some" truth to John, Jane, and Adam's statements.

Phone calls and texts with Adam became fewer and fewer. I was in the dark. Every conversation Adam and I had either by phone or text message was always good. We did not talk about things that would cause emotions to rise. The picture that Adam had painted of me was awful. I couldn't believe that my own child could be that deceptive with me. Why did I not see it? Was I really that blind this whole time? I never wanted Adam to be in harm's way but I was losing this battle, and I knew it.

> Evil is bad sold as good, wrong sold as right, injustice sold as justice. Like the coat of a virus, a thin veil of right can disguise enormous wrong and confer an ability to infect others."
> — John Hartung

John had filed for Sole Custody of our son. I wasn't shocked about this latest filing. Honestly, how could I be? In reading these documents I was again hit with the frustration and anger. I decided that this time, I wanted to hear from the "horse's mouth". I called our son, who was 15 years old at the time.

When he answered there was a level of disrespect that was insurmountable. I was immediately in shock. Where was this coming from? I explained to Adam that his Dad had filed another motion for Sole Custody, with zero contact with me. Adam explained that he knew about it. I asked him, *"Is this what you want?"*. Adam replied, *"For now."* I explained to Adam that this was not a "for now" thing, that this was permanent and that I would see him when I saw him. He said, *"That's fine"*. I explained to Adam that he needed to start accepting his own accountability, he became angry and lashed out. I told Adam that I don't know what "wrong" he believed I had done to him, but I go to bed every night with a clear conscious and I asked him if he could as well. He didn't answer. I told him that I loved him. We hung up the phone and my mom looked at me, I looked at her and said, *"I'm done, he isn't worth saving and I don't know if he ever was."*

Adam had no idea that his grandmother had heard every word he said and the disrespect in his voice. This would become important later on. This was the last time I had spoken to Adam.

I contacted my attorney and told her to *"give John what he wants, there's no point in fighting over someone who wants absolutely nothing to do with me"*.

26. 2840 - Ord Denying ...	05-Dec-2014	*Extra Text: ORDER DENYING EX PARTE EMERGENCY MOTION REGARDING CHILDREN - Transaction 4722276 - Approved By: NOREVIEW : 12-05-2014:08:35:46*
30. 1695 - ** Exhibit(s) ...	18-Sep-2014	*Extra Text: 09/18/14 EX PARTE*
31. 2645 - Opposition to Mtn ...	15-Sep-2014	*Extra Text: OPPOSITION TO EX PARTE EMERGENCY MOTION REGARDING CHILDREN*
33. 3242 - Ord Setting Hearing	11-Sep-2014	*Extra Text: Transaction 4602323 - Approved By: NOREVIEW : 09-11-2014:13:49:11*
35. 3860 - Request for Submission	05-Sep-2014	*Extra Text: Transaction 4594086 - Approved By: CKOEHLER : 09-05-2014:15:19:18 DOCUMENT TITLE: SUSPEND CONTACT AND VISITATION FROM BIO MOTHER (NO PAPER ORDER PROVIDED) PARTY SUBMITTING: JOHN DOE DATE SUBMITTED: SEPTEMBER 5, 2014 SUBMITTED BY: CKOEHLER DATE RECEIVED JUDGE OFFICE:*
37. $1985 - **$Motion/Opposition Notice	05-Sep-2014	*Extra Text:*
40. 4300 - Withdrawal of Counsel	26-Aug-2014	*Extra Text: CARL WILLIAM HART, III, ESQ / JOHN DOE Transaction 4577486 - Approved By: MCHOLICO : 08-26-2014:13:16:04*

CHAPTER 13

2015

Judge Cynthia Lu granted John's motion for sole custody. It was ordered that I have absolutely no contact with Adam. I was hurt, I sent John a text message stating to both him and Adam to leave me alone. I no longer have a son.

A short time later, Adam texted his grandmother saying that since he no longer has a mother, he no longer has grandparents either. Everything that I tried so hard to avoid was happening. John had managed to isolate his son and succeed in by far the worst case of parental alienation I have seen.

> "I guess that's just part of loving people: You have to give things up. Sometimes you even have to give them up."
> — Lauren Oliver, Delirium

Child Support

In August 2015, I attended a hearing regarding the child support issue via telephone. This hearing was about two cases. The Washoe County District Attorney's Office was handling my case regarding John's arrears. The State of Nevada was handling John's case against me. The issue started a few years back when the State of Nevada began offsetting my income tax returns and garnishing my paychecks.

The child support order was clear, my child support was set at $100.00 per month. This amount would be deducted from John's arrears. When his arrears were paid, then collection of actual monies would begin. The State of Nevada ignored this order and began collection of child support. During this time, John was free and clear, not having to pay his arrears. I contacted the Washoe County District Attorney's Office regarding this issue. I was told that they were not in charge of this case, that I needed to contact the State of Nevada regarding this issue. I contacted my attorney. She sent a letter explaining the order and that they needed to stop immediately from collecting support or file a motion to modify. We waited for their reply, it never came.

I received a notice of intent to suspend my driver's license for non-payment of support. How is this even possible? I contacted my attorney immediately. She sent another letter explaining the order once again. No reply.

I was informed that John had requested a hearing to modify the child support. The audacity of this, here we have a father who for years did not pay any child support. Who for years, did not pay the full amount. He was never met with any consequences. He never had his driver's license suspended, no tax return offsets, nothing. Yet, he wanted to modify the child support order, which all in all was benefitting him more than me! He was not responsible for the arrears, he did not have to pay anything. Just have his son, raise him, and be a parent for once. He was not happy with this.

The audacity of the State of Nevada to send me such a notice, knowing full well that they were violating a court order is insurmountable.

I received a Notice of Intent to Enforce and Modify from the State of Nevada Division of Welfare and Supportive Services. It was stated that on "September 9, 2012 I was ordered to pay $100.00 per month, a copy of this child support order is attached." There was no child support order attached. The document went on to say that "It is alleged by the Obligee (John) that you are in arrears on behalf of your child in the amount of $1,023.10 through November 30, 2014." I scoured through my pile of court documents and found the Stipulation and Order RE: Modification of Child Custody, Visitation, Child Support & Insurance for Minor Child.

This order was dated September 20, 2012. The date on their Intent to Enforce and Modify would not be the only error on the State of Nevada's part. The Child Support order states clearly:

"c. Meghan shall be ordered to pay child support in the amount of $100.00 per month, due and payable on the first day of each month. Until such time as the child support arrearage owed by John to

Meghan are satisfied in full, Washoe County shall keep an accounting demonstrating the reduction of the outstanding arrearage and shall not deliver payment in monies to John. After such time as the termination of parental rights is entered by the court, the child support obligation shall cease. If the court fails to terminate the parental rights of Meghan, then once the child support arrearage is satisfied in full, Meghan shall pay child support in the amount of $100.00 per month, all payments will be through Washoe County District Attorney."

The big question was, how do I have arrears for child support that according to the current child support order I don't even owe? I decided to go through my paperwork and find every document showing what had been garnished from my paychecks and offset from my income tax returns.

I gathered all this information and sent it to my attorney. How can the State of Nevada violate a court order and then tell me that I owe arrears? This was all beyond my comprehension. My attorney filed an Opposition to the Motion to Modify Child Support. In this opposition, there were several exhibits included. Of course, the stipulation and child support order in addition to the documents showing garnishment of paychecks, offsets for tax returns and arrears still owed by John. It is interesting to note that while the State of Nevada was collecting child support from me, there were no actions to collect the arrears from John.

Because of several health issues and attendance, I was terminated from my job with the United States Post Office. At the time of the hearing, my attorney had mentioned to the judge that I had not been working since July 29, 2015. When I was finally going to be officially terminated, I informed my attorney. She put together a motion to modify the child support and submitted it to the courts on November 30, 2015.

I contacted Derrick Bailey and explained to him that I had not been working since July 29, 2015. I told him that I was requesting a modification of my child support since my income had dropped well below $100.00 per month. In fact, I was bringing in a whopping $0.00. I received a notice from the State of Nevada that stated I had requested a modification, I was to provide a financial disclosure statement to them. I filled that out and sent it back.

I received another notice from the State of Nevada stating that my request to modify my child support was approved and that 18% of my gross income right now was $0.00. In this letter is stated that I could contact their office and speak with Derrick Bailey to see if we could come to some sort of agreement, if no agreement could be reached then a hearing would be set on this matter and I would then be notified of the hearing date and time.

I received an email from my attorney asking me if it was ok for her to contact Derrick Bailey and see if some sort of agreement could be made. Of course, I said yes. I received an email back stating that she had talked with Derrick Bailey and that she felt that this was going to go to a hearing. She stated that Derrick would "talk" with John about reducing my child support back down to $100.00 per month.

1. 2700 - Ord After Hearing...	11-Jun-2015	*Extra Text: Transaction 4996218 - Approved By: NOREVIEW : 06-11-2015:16:03:28*
6. 3370 - Order ...	20-Apr-2015	*Extra Text: ORDER TO APPEAR - Transaction 4914085 - Approved By: NOREVIEW : 04-20-2015:11:01:51*
7. 3860 - Request for Submission	24-Mar-2015	*Extra Text: MOTION FOR FULL SOLE PHYSICAL/LEGAL CUSTODY OF MINOR (PAPER ORDER NOT PROVIDED) - Transaction 4875800 - Approved By: KJONES : 03-24-2015:14:43:18 PARTY SUBMITTING: JOHN DOE DATE SUBMITTED: MARCH 24, 2015 SUBMITTED BY: KJONES DATE RECEIVED JUDGE OFFICE:*
8. 3790 - Reply to/in Opposition	24-Mar-2015	*Extra Text: REPLY TO OPPOSITION TO MOTION - Transaction 4875800 - Approved By: KJONES : 03-24-2015:14:43:18*
13. 2645 - Opposition to Mtn ...	19-Mar-2015	*Extra Text: OPPOSITION TO DEFENDANT'S MOTION RE: EXERCISE OF JURISDICTION OF THIS COURTOVER A CHILD WHO IS NOT INVOLVED IN THIS CASE*
15. $1985 - **$Motion/Opposition Notice	19-Mar-2015	*Extra Text:*
17. 2490 - Motion ...	06-Mar-2015	*Extra Text:*
19. $1985 - **$Motion/Opposition Notice	06-Mar-2015	*Extra Text:*
22. 3860 - Request for Submission	15-Jan-2015	*Extra Text: DOCUMENT TITLE: PROPOSED ORDER AFTER HEARING PARTY SUBMITTING: JOHN DOE DATE SUBMITTED: 01/15/15 SUBMITTED BY: MPURDY*

for KJONES DATE RECEIVED JUDGE OFFICE:

CHAPTER 14

2016

My Driver's License had been suspended on February 15, 2016 for nonpayment of child support. During this time, there was no word from the State of Nevada or my attorney regarding an agreement or a hearing on the matter. All the while, the arrears are going up. The state of Nevada was more than eager to file for a motion to modify based on the inaccuracies of John's statement. They were even more eager to file a motion to modify a child support order that they clearly violated and stole money from me. But, while I am unemployed and being completely honest with them, I cannot get a hearing for a modification which based on the statutes is my absolute right. Instead, my driver's license is suspended and I am stuck with ever increasing arrears.

It is clear that the original child support order was more beneficial for both John and myself, since no money would be taken out. His arrears being over $7,000.00 would mean that he would never have to pay me the money back. I had raised Adam on minimal if any child support since he was a year and a half old. John had been raising Adam since he was 11 years old without child support. There were no complaints from either one of us.

We finally got a hearing on this matter. Master Greg Shannon would be presiding over this. As I walked in, I immediately knew this was not going to go in my favor. My attorney had prepared several documents to serve as proof of my claim that I was unable to work because of medical issues. When she tried to submit those to the court, Master Shannon refused them. He wanted a note from a Doctor that specifically said that I could not work. The hospital records, the various other proof that I was unable to perform my job were not sufficient in his eyes.

He ordered that child support be in the amount of $435.00 per month. My attorney argued that this was ridiculous at best, how could an unemployed person pay that amount of child support? Logic seemed to escape this court.

The idiocy of this is insurmountable. The $25.00 that John is ordered to pay is the only income that I had. That in turn goes back to the State of Nevada for my child support. Thus, no one is really paying any child support or arrears. It is a never-ending circle of idiocy brought on by the State of Nevada.

As soon as I was terminated and received a letter and more medical records from Physical Therapy and my primary doctor, my attorney filed for another hearing on this matter. By this time, I was more so limping into the court room. The letter did not "specifically" say that I could not go to work, but did in fact detail the issues I was having and the need for various medications which left me impaired. THIS was not enough for the court. While the State of Nevada was able to submit their evidence into court, my due process rights were completely ignored. Instead, Master Shannon had ordered that I was willfully underemployed and that I could come back again once I had a letter that was specific to his request. This did not sit well with my attorney, she filed for a Trial de Novo with the District Judge.

Judge Humke would receive this appeal and would later request all the medical documents we had tried to submit previously, but he also wanted two personal statements from me. I was more than happy to comply.

On June 02, 2016, I was involved in a motor vehicle accident. Later it was discovered that I had suffered Bilateral Vertebral Artery Dissections and developed a blood clot. I would end up being life flighted to the University of Utah Hospital in Salt Lake City, Utah where I would spend approximately 4 days. I was released to come home, with my own little pharmacy in tow we had thought the worst was behind us.

Two weeks after I returned home, I had suffered a severe dizzy spell and collapsed into my Fiancé's arms. The ambulance was called and I was again life flighted to the University of Utah Hospital. I underwent several MRI's and tests, I continued to have bouts of severe dizziness. On August 07, 2016, I suffered a Right Lateral Medullary Stroke and Basilar Artery Occlusion. While I should have just been focused on recovery, the child support issue was still in the air.

On March 27, 2017, I finally got the justice I had been fighting for. I had not heard back from my attorney regarding our appeal to the district judge. I decided that it didn't matter to me what this court decided. The injustice I had experienced for years left me with zero hope that anything would go right. I simply did not care, what were they going to do, take away my birthday?

We finally got another hearing on this matter. The Attorney General Tammy Tovey-Stephenson walked down the little hallway and gave a quick smile to John outside the courtroom. As she turned my direction, it was a look of contempt. We were called into the courtroom. I walked in as best I could with my cane and a steady arm nearby. Court was called to order. I knew my tremors were going to take over, one of the deficits of my strokes is that I am unable to process emotions like normal. When I get anxious or nervous my tremors tend to get worse. Sitting there next to my attorney with her caring hand on my back attempting to soothe me, I broke down in tears. I was sobbing uncontrollably. I couldn't believe what John and the Attorney General were saying.

Watching me there, shaking uncontrollably, they still had the audacity to act as if I had been faking this all along. At one-point John had stated *"Her disabilities are no worse than my own."* As he stood there, upright and steady he tried to argue that I had been released to go back to work, insisting that is what the doctor's letter had stated. There was one point where surely, they had to be able to see what this man was all about and how ridiculous his claims were. I thought that point was when he blurted out *"I don't know how she got a Handicap Placard, she can't even drive!"*

John pleaded with the courts saying *"My son graduates in 3 months and then he'll be 18, I won't get any help! I haven't gotten any help in a couple years!"*

The Attorney General went to an even more petty argument stating that the letter from my Rehabilitation Doctor in Salt Lake City was not good enough because he did not have "M.D."

behind his name. It almost sounded as if she implied that these strokes were "convenient" when she said *"Well, why did it take so long for a doctor to say she was disabled?"*. I couldn't help but sit there awe struck. ALL OF THIS because I had become unemployed and couldn't work. Two years of litigating the fact that I was unemployed and according to statute automatically granted me a modification. I wasn't asking to be forgiven the total amount of child support, but just be fair. How could anyone pay $435.00 a month in child support if they were unemployed and unable to collect unemployment benefits?

In the end, the Court Master did follow the District Judge's recommendation. I was ordered to pay $100.00 a month plus $25.00 a month for arrears. It was painfully obvious that no one would ever see a dime from me. But, it must be in writing to satisfy any legalities.

Vindication came when my attorney printed up the Recommendation. As I read through it in her office, the tears came again. This time, it was happiness and relief. Finally, someone saw the injustice that was occurring in that court room.

1 Obligor filed the requested information with the Court for its consideration in ruling on
2 the motions for reconsideration and for trial de novo.

3   Having reviewed the record, the Court finds and orders as follows:

4   FINDINGS OF FACT

5   <u>Two Page Statement Explaining the Termination of Employment</u>

6   On October 17, 2016 Obligor submitted a supplement pursuant to Court order of
7 September 16, 2016 - attached as Exhibit 1 was Obligor's two page statement explaining
8 her inability to sustain full time employment. This Court has reviewed Obligor's
9 statement and recognizes Obligor was experiencing medical problems that impacted her
10 ability to fulfill her full time employment obligations at USPS. Additionally, the Court
11 recognizes Obligor was involved in a motor vehicle accident resulting in significant
12 medical problems requiring intensive care and therapy. Under these circumstances, the
13 Court finds sustaining full-time employment at USPS would have been difficult at best.
14 Following the motor vehicle accident the Court finds Obligors ability to work even part-
15 time would be impossible. Based upon Obligors statements, the Court finds good cause to
16 reconsider the Master's recommendations to modify filed July 5, 2016.

16 reconsider the Master's recommendations to modify filed July 5, 2016.
17   <u>Medical Records Supporting Illnesses and Medications taken by Obligor for Health</u>
18   <u>Issues during the time period July 26, 2016 - May 11, 2016.</u>
19   On October 17, 2016 Obligor submitted a supplement pursuant to Court order of
20 September 16, 2016 - attached as Exhibit 2 were Obligor's medical records relevant to the
21 July 26, 2015 - May 11, 2016 time period. The Court has reviewed the submitted medical
22 records and finds Obligor was treated for significant dental problems on July 26, 2015
23 wherein she was prescribed medication including narcotic pain pills which affect one's
24 ability to operative machinery due to the side effects of drowsiness, dizziness and delayed
25 response time.

26   Thereafter, on August 13, 2015, Obligor underwent dental surgery requiring
27 anesthesia wherein Obligor had three abscessed teeth removed as a result of large carious
28 lesions being discovered. Post operation Obligor was prescribed medication included

1 narcotic pain pills. Despite taken the prescribed antibiotic based medication Obligor
2 continued to experience oral infections. Consequently, on September 10, 2015, Obligor
3 underwent oral surgery requiring anesthesia wherein Obligor had an additional three
4 teeth extracted. Post operation Obligor was again prescribed narcotic pain medication.
5   Obligor's medical records in Exhibit 2 continue from November 23, 2015 - May 11,
6 2015 wherein she is treated for a variety of ailments including musculoskeletal pain of
7 which she was prescribed pain medication and physical therapy.
8   Upon review of these records; specifically, the dental records, the Court is satisfied
9 that Obligor experienced significant health challenges that prevented her from fulfilling
10 her full-time work obligations with USPS which ultimately resulted in her termination of
11 employment on December 5, 2015.

3   In reviewing Obligor's written statement in conjunction with Obligor's medical
4 records its clear Obligor's physical and mental limitations prevented and continue to
5 prevent Obligor from sustaining employment at this time.

CONCLUSION OF LAW

7   In this case, Obligor has requested reconsideration of Master's findings and
8 recommendations; additionally, in the alternative Obligor has requested a trial de novo. In
9 the interest of judicial economy, this Court addresses the issues presented to it under a
0 motion for reconsideration framework.

In this case, the Court finds reconsideration justified as a result of newly discovered evidence not previously available and for the need to prevent manifest injustice. As noted in this Court's September 16, 2016 order, the Court shared the same concern as the Court Master did upon hearing the limited evidence presented to it. Consequently, this Court asked Obligor to submit supplemental evidence to substantiate her physical and mental difficulties that has prevented her from working.

Upon review of the supplemental information as outlined above, the Court finds the newly discovered evidence requires this Court to reconsider the Court Master's findings and recommendations. Furthermore, failing to reconsider the Court Master's findings and recommendation would result in a manifest injustice towards the Obligor.

Specifically, the Court finds Obligor underwent significant dental treatment on July 26, 2015, August 13, 2015 and September 10, 2015. Following each of these treatment dates Obligor was prescribed narcotic pain medication which interfered with her ability to carry out fulltime employment with USPS. Consequently, Obligor was provided notice on November 2, 2015 that she would be terminated from her position at USPS on December 5, 2015.

(1996). In this case, the Court cites Obligor's motion to modify / reduce child support filed on November 30, 2015 as the most prudent date to apply the Court's reconsideration. Accordingly, the Court finds as of December 5, 2015 till the date in which this order was filed, Obligor has been unable sustain employment as a direct result of the medical conditions she has suffered from.

Based upon the foregoing, Obligor's Motion for Reconsideration is hereby GRANTED. Pursuant to NRS 125B.140(1)(b) and NRS 125B.080 this Court's directs the Court Master to consider retroactively modifying Obligor's child support obligations to the statutory minimum of $100.00 as of December 5, 2015.

ORDER DIRECTING COURT MASTER TO CONSIDER RETROACTIVELY MODIFYING CHILD SUPPORT AT UPCOMING MODIFICATION HEARING

On January 17, 2017, the Court Master filed an order setting Obligor's motion to modify/reduce child support for a hearing. Thereafter, on January 26, 2017 a notice to set was filed wherein the parties were directed to meet on February 2, 2017 at 9:30 a.m., to set a hearing date for Obligor's motion. Accordingly, the Court directs the parties to proceed forward in setting a hearing on the motion wherein the Court Master shall consider retroactively modifying Obligor's child support obligations in conformity with this order. Specifically, the Court Master shall consider retroactively modifying Obligor's child support obligations to the statutory minimum of $100.00 dollars as of December 5, 2015.

Additionally, this Court directs the Court Master consider recalculating Obligor's child support arrearages in conformity with Obligor's child support obligation being set at the statutory minimum of $100.00 as of December 5, 2015.

Clear to this Court is Obligor's inability to sustain fulltime employment as of June 2, 2016, which is the date she was involved in a motor vehicle accident until the present time. Additionally, clear to this Court is on December 5, 2015, Obligor was not willfully unemployed as she was terminated as a direct result of medical complications that interfered with her ability to perform work tasks at USPS.

This Court does grant the Court Master discretion in determining Obligor's ability to work from the time period of December 5, 2015 – June 2, 2016. In reviewing the record,

this Court does recognize Obligor was experiencing mild to moderate medical challenges that could interfere with her ability to work on a fulltime basis. Additionally, Obligor had her driver license suspended on or about April 27, 2016 which would have limited her ability to compete for employment positions similar to her duties performed at USPS.

Accordingly, the Court Master is granted discretion to determine the appropriate child support obligations during the December 5, 2015 – June 2, 2015 time period if the evidence presented to him indicates the statutory minimum of $100.00 is not warranted

GOOD CAUSE APPEARING, IT IS SO ORDERED.

Dated: February ___, 2017.

_____
District Judge

On July 18, 2017, I received a call from Joyce at the Washoe County District Attorney's office, she left a message stating that she wanted to discuss my case against John. On July 19, 2017, I spoke with Joyce. Apparently, John had contacted them and wants to make a deal. He would forgive the amount I owe him for child support if I were to forgive the amount he owes me. Since my attorney is handling the case with the State of Nevada, I couldn't say much on that, I don't see where John would have any authority to grant forgiveness. I explained to Joyce that this matter had already been discussed and ordered on in a hearing that took place on March 27, 2017.

It was made very clear that neither the State of Nevada or John would ever get a dime from me considering the severity of my disabilities, in addition to them being scolded by the District Judge for their previous ludicrous actions in past hearings. While discussing this with Joyce, I told her that as far as my case against John, their office has not done their job in enforcing this case in years and I have already accepted that I will never see the arrears that John owes. Zero out the balance, I don't care, I just want him GONE. She would contact me in a few days and let me know what the decision would be.

I received the stipulations on August 9, 2017. My attorney gladly looked over them and made sure that this was going to be the end. Although John would have others believe the worst and that I was a deadbeat mom, once the final amounts were given, I only owed the State of Nevada $7.89. John would still owe me a difference of $2,054.15. I was given the opportunity to still collect that difference, but would it be worth it? No.

18	2. A judgment is entered against Obligor for child
19	support arrears in the amount of $5,507.76 in principal plus
20	$1,642.37 in interest plus $430.19 in penalties for a total of
21	$7,580.32 from July 1, 2015 through July 31, 2017. (see attached
22	Custodian Financial Audit). Obligee knowingly and voluntarily
23	agreed to waive the arrears including interest and penalties
24	through July 31, 2017.

1	3.	Obligee, ███████████████ knowingly and willingly waives his portion of		
2		arrears for the period of **March 1, 2017** through **July 31, 2017** as follows:		
3		Principal:	$4,348.10	
4		Interest:	$ 457.25	
5		Penalty:	$ 720.82	
6		Total:	$5,526.17	
7	4.	A judgment is entered in favor of The Division of Welfare and Supportive Services for		
8		the period of **March 1, 2017** through **July 31, 2017** as follows:		
9		Principal:	$0.00	
10		Interest:	$7.89	
11		Penalty:	$0.00	
		Total:	$7.89	

This was the end of it all.

In total, through 17 years of litigation and numerous court hearings, there were 6 different judges that handled this court case. Every time the case would get a new judge, they would not look back at the extensive history of this case, instead they would make their orders based on the present filings at hand. Leaving Adam's safety and well-being in jeopardy. The courts claim that they act in the best interests of the child, but allow this type of viciousness to overtake their courtrooms. It is a tragedy for all divorce cases that involve children.

"There is no greater tyranny than that which is perpetrated under the shield of the law and in the name of justice."
— Charles-Louis de Secondat, de la Brède et de Montesquieu, The Spirit of the Laws

On July 20, 2017, Adam turned 18 years old. John was so consumed with anger and raw hatred for me, that he managed to torment me for 18 years of his life. So focused on hurting me and spewing such lies, what, if anything has he gained in the end?

Only he can really answer that. I however have gained a whole new insight into the Family Court System. My own strength and endurance to fight for what is right, seeing people for who and what they are, and seeing just how vile some people can be even when they "swear" it is all for the child. I have managed to save my daughter from such an ill fate by working for the best relationship between her father and myself and throwing aside all the hurt, anger, pain that was caused by that marriage. I have found myself in the process. I have made the ultimate sacrifice that a mother could make, all for the love and what she hoped was the well-being of her child.

It has been two years since I have spoken to Adam. After the last conversation, the lies he told to those at West Hills and his counselors, and after disowning his grandparents… I'm not sure that I do want to speak with him. There is so much negativity surrounding this, with all that I have gone through and my own recovery, I cannot allow that seed of negativity into my life. My daughter and I deserve better.

I think of him often, I even pray for him nightly… I will always love him, he is my son and a piece of my heart will always be gone. But the truth is, who he is now… I don't know him and in turn he doesn't know me.

Remember… don't let the hatred of other's change you…I pray that you find your happiness, wherever that may be… I love you

"Injustice anywhere is a threat to justice everywhere."
― Martin Luther King, Jr.